Essential Guide to Scrapbooking

Essential Guide to Scrapbooking
Editor: Carrie E. Holcomb
Contributing Editor: Sue M. Banker
Associate Design Director: Som Inthalangsy
Contributing Designer: Craig Hanken, Studio P2
Copy Chief: Terri Fredrickson
Publishing Operations Manager: Karen Schirm
Senior Editor, Asset and Information Manager: Phillip Morgan
Edit and Design Production Coordinator: Mary Lee Gavin
Editorial Assistant: Cheryl Eckert
Book Production Managers: Pam Kvitne, Marjorie J. Schenkelberg, Rick von Holdt, Mark Weaver
Contributing Proofreader: Heidi Johnson

Meredith® Books
Executive Director, Editorial: Gregory H. Kayko
Executive Director, Design: Matt Strelecki
Managing Editor: Amy Tincher-Durik
Senior Editor/Group Manager: Jan Miller
Senior Associate Design Director: Ken Carlson
Marketing Product Manager: Gina Rickert

Publisher and Editor in Chief: James D. Blume
Editorial Director: Linda Raglan Cunningham
Executive Director, New Business Development: Todd M. Davis
Executive Director, Sales: Ken Zagor
Director, Operations: George A. Susral
Director, Production: Douglas M. Johnston
Director, Marketing: Amy Nichols
Business Director: Jim Leonard

Vice President and General Manager: Douglas J. Guendel

Better Homes and Gardens® Magazine
Editor in Chief; Karol DeWulf Nickell

Meredith Publishing Group
President: Jack Griffin
Executive Vice President: Bob Mate

Meredith Corporation
Chairman and Chief Executive Officer: William T. Kerr
President and Chief Operating Officer: Stephen M. Lacy

In Memoriam: E.T. Meredith III (1933-2003)

First Edition.

ISBN: 0-696-23303-7

All of us at Better Homes and Gardens® Books are dedicated to providing you with the information and ideas to create beautiful and useful projects. We welcome your comments and suggestions. Write to us at: Better Homes and Gardens Books, Crafts Editorial Department, 1716 Locust St., Des Moines, IA 50309-3023.

If you would like to purchase any of our crafts, cooking, gardening, home improvement, or home decorating and design books, check wherever quality books are sold. Or visit us at: bhgbooks.com

Excerpted from *Better Homes and Gardens® Fast Scrapbooking* and *Better Homes and Gardens® Scrapbooking.* Also published as Borders at Home *Essential Guide to Scrapbooking.*

Pictured on the back cover: Top left: Grandpa's Music, page 250; Top right: Camping, page 180; Bottom left: Marching Band, page 66; Bottom right: Our Dog T-Bone, page 123.

make it memorable

OK, let's admit it—we all wish our treasured photos were anywhere but tucked away in a box for no one to enjoy. Those photos, along with cherished bits and pieces of memorabilia, are the layers of our lives.

As scrapbooking fanatics, our biggest dream is to dust off those memory-filled boxes and transfer the contents into work-of-art scrapbook albums we'll be proud to share.

Within this book you'll find all the scrapbooking information and inspiration to do just that. You'll discover hundreds of pages that will spark ideas for your own. Tips to make the process easier, no fail, and quick to achieve. You'll be encouraged to try new products, approaches, and techniques—all of which you can master in no time.

What if you're new to the scrapbooking craze? No problem! The glossary will introduce you to the terms, tools, and supplies.

To get you started we have included wonderful artwork for you to photocopy and use: papers, mats, corners—everything you need to create pages that look like a million dollars.

So get out those sacred pieces of paper and enjoy sharing the stories of your life.

Carrie E. Holcomb

Carrie E. Holcomb, Editor

contents

FUN
at the
LAKE
day at...
Mall of America!
LEGOLAND

how to use this book

All in one convenient book—
YOU'LL LEARN
- which supplies to get and how to use them
- tips to make great-looking pages, plus a glossary to clarify the terminology

YOU'LL GET
- materials lists and helpful pointers to re-create each sample page
- exclusive papers, headlines, and quotes to make scrapbooking easy

For those new to scrapbooking or those who have been cropping for years, this book reviews the tools, tips, and techniques needed for successful scrapbooking and provides oodles of ideas to make wonderful pages. For a basic review of tools and supplies, check out *pages 8–17*. Grab some tips from the scrapping experts on *pages 18–21*. And scour the scrapbooking terms in the glossary on *pages 262–265* to help you along the way.

Making the Pages

To help you reproduce the hundreds of scrapbook page samples in this book, each scrapbook page includes an overview of how the page was created, a quick tip, a materials list, and pointers to guide you through the process.

1 The Overview

The paragraph at the top of each page gives a brief explanation of the strategy of the page. Step-by-step instructions will be included here for any complicated steps.

2 The Quick Tip

A circular closeup highlights a detail from the page and gives a tip to make creating the feature quick and easy.

3 The Materials List

The side column includes a complete list of the scrapbooking supplies used to make the page. Starting with photos or other artistic creations, the list continues with papers, embellishments, tools, and adhesives.

emma and honey

Make it in minutes with copy, cut, and use photo frames. These

1 coordinating frames are provided on *pages 313* and *317*. Cut them out and layer them on additional papers to make the page rich with color.

2 QUICK TIP

Use a loop of gold jumpring to hang a paper tag from ½-inch-wide ribbon.

3 **materials**

- photos
- 12-inch square of green polka-dot paper
- rust subtle-pattern scrapbook paper
- dark green card stock
- color photocopy of mats and tag, pages 313 and 317
- ½-inch-wide gold and burgundy ribbon
- gold jumpring
- paper punch
- paper trimmer
- black marking pen
- crafts knife
- adhesive

Art in back of book!

see pages 313 and 317

Punch a hole in the top edge of the tag. Thread ribbon through a jumpring; attach the tag.

Fold ribbon back and forth vertically on the page, adhering in spots with glue stick.

Trim a wider green mat to back the provided decorative mat. Cut out the frame center using a crafts knife.

4

129

4 The Callouts

At the bottom of each page, a line links captions to the related area of the sample scrapbook page to clarify how to construct the page.

5 Art or Pattern in Back of Book!

When you see this circular image, find the corresponding scrapbooking artwork printed in the back of the book. This section includes frames, borders, and other decorative details to photocopy and use.

And there's more!

Instant Headlines

You'll find several quick headlines at the end of each chapter. To have these headlines on hand, make several photocopies and keep them in a large envelope. Permission is given in the front of the book to photocopy these headlines for personal use.

Quick Journaling

Throughout the book you'll discover dozens of ways to journal. When you're at a loss for what to say, use these tips to find inspiration in a jiffy:

- Use personal or famous quotes *(see page 40)*
- Use dictionary definitions *(see page 42)*
- Use preprinted materials, such as newspaper clippings or brochures *(see pages 54–55)*
- Take notes or keep a journal when taking photographs

gather your supplies

Getting started is half the fun of scrapbooking. Just walk into any scrapbooking store and find yourself wonderfully lost in a paradise of gorgeous papers, intricate die-cuts and stickers, punches and stamps of every imaginable shape, a counter full of adhesives, and embellishments pretty enough to wear. The supply options open to scrapbookers are amazing, and that makes the shopping awesome!

Supplies used to make the scrapbook pages in this book are listed below and through *page 13.* Keep these items on hand to scrapbook whenever your schedule allows. Because time is often an issue for scrapbookers, tips are provided so you can spend less time at the store and more time making beautifully memorable pages!

Many of the sample scrapbook pages in this book use the following supplies:

Adhesive Mesh

Adhesive Mesh

This adhesive-backed mesh is plastic and is available in a range of widths and colors. Placed on a scrapbook page, the mesh creates a gridded texture.

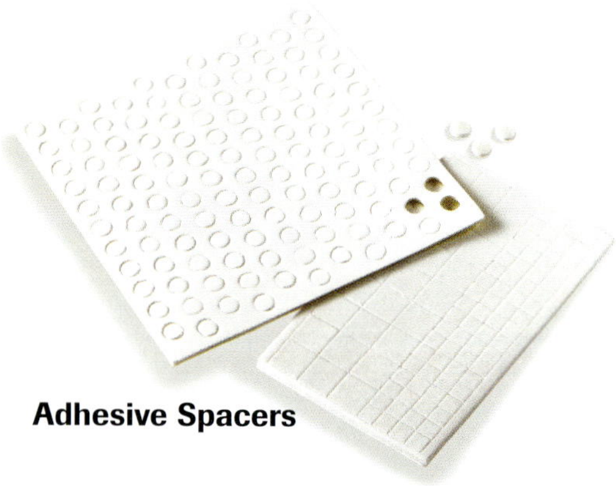

Adhesive Spacers

Adhesive Spacers

These adhesives are packaged in rolls or sheets. Varying in size, shape, and thickness, the spacers hold papers together as well as raise a paper layer from the background.

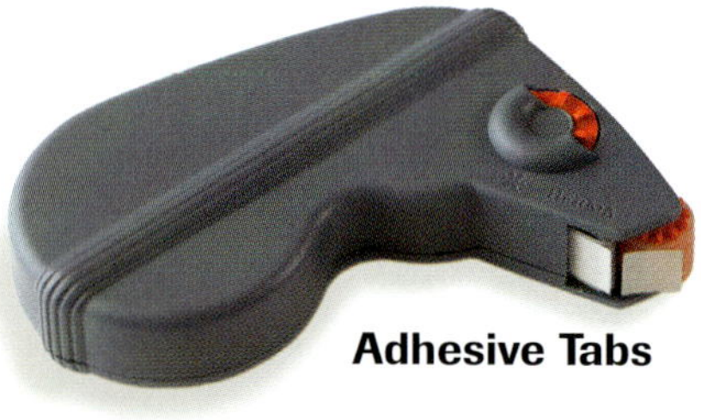

Adhesive Tabs

Adhesive Tabs

This type of adhesive is used mainly to adhere papers, including photos. Tabs come on a roll in an easy-to-use applicator.

Alphabet and Word Stickers

Available in a gamut of styles from playful to refined, these stickers give journaling, headlines, and labels a professional look.

Alphabet and Word Stickers

Brads

Scrapbooking stores offer decorative brads that contribute instant detail to pages. Each brad has two prongs on the back that insert through paper(s) and then bend outward and flat to to secure the paper in place. The mini trims are available in several shapes and colors.

Brads

Corner Scissors

These scissors transform a right-angle corner into a decorative shape. The blades have guides for positioning the paper before cutting. Some brands offer more than one cutting choice, such as the pictured pair of scissors, which features four options.

Corner Scissors

Decorating Chalk

While sidewalk chalk smears or rubs off after application, this type is more permanent. Decorating chalk is available in a rainbow of colors at scrapbooking and stamping stores. Apply it with your finger or the applicator that comes with the chalk.

Decorating Chalk

Decorative-Edge Scissors

Decorative-Edge Scissors

Available in many different styles, decorative-edge scissors enable a scrapbooker to trim paper so it has a repeating pattern on the edge.

Die-Cuts

Die-Cuts

die-cuts are paper shapes that can be simple or intricate in design. Some purchased die-cuts use layering to develop the design's detail. Those shown here have detailed laser cuts to give them a realistic appearance. Or make your own die-cuts using punches or templates.

Dimensional Stickers

Dimensional Stickers

These fun theme stickers are miniature representations of the real thing. The adhesive-backed stickers are created from a variety of materials, including fabric, paper, and plastic, and often have such details as beads and glitter.

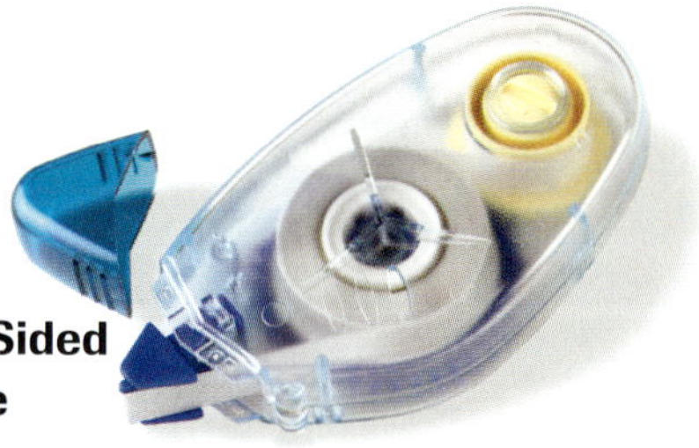

Double-Sided Adhesive

Double-Sided Adhesive

Available in the form of tape, several brands are available for scrapbooking. The style shown here is permanent and tacky enough to hold micro beads and comes in a roll dispenser.

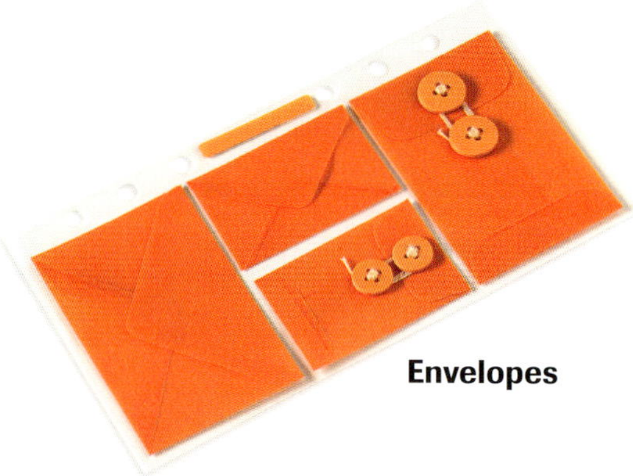

Envelopes

Envelopes

Charming embellishments that work for many scrapbook layouts, envelopes are made in several sizes, colors, and papers. Shown here are small vellum envelopes with traditional flap and button-wrap closures.

Eyelet Tools

Two types of eyelet tools are available. One is a handheld setter that resembles a paper punch. The other type includes an eyelet setter (small metal rod), a protective mat, and a hammer.

Eyelet Setters

Eyelets

Made from thin metal, eyelets are usually pea-size, but larger ones also are available. When used for scrapbooking they hold papers together, create a hole for threading fiber, or accent a feature of the page.

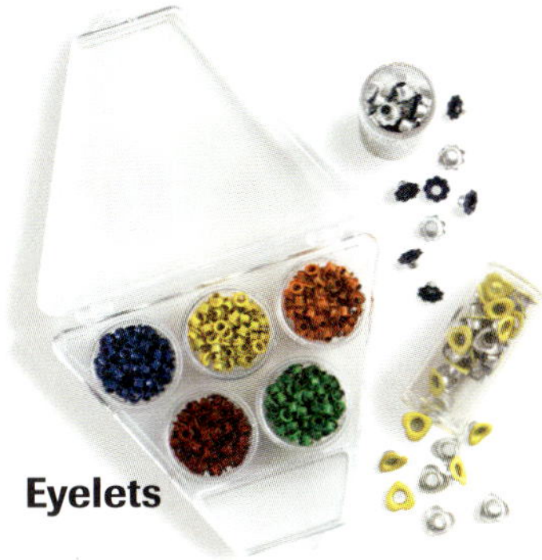

Eyelets

Fibers

Available in a variety of colors, textures, and lengths, these threads usually are sold as an assortment on cards and are used to enhance scrapbooking pages.

Fibers

File

A handy accessory for scrapbooking, this case has divided sections in which to store papers or pages until they are put in an album.

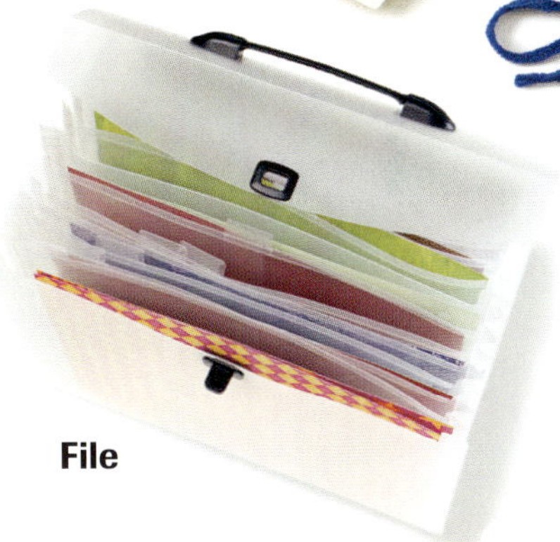

File

Glue Sticks

These adhesives are encased in tubes. Some of this type of glue is temporary, allowing you to reposition the item being glued. Use it along paper edges or in corners.

Glue Sticks

Marking Pens

Available in a rainbow of colors and widths, these pens are used often for journaling or coloring in small details.

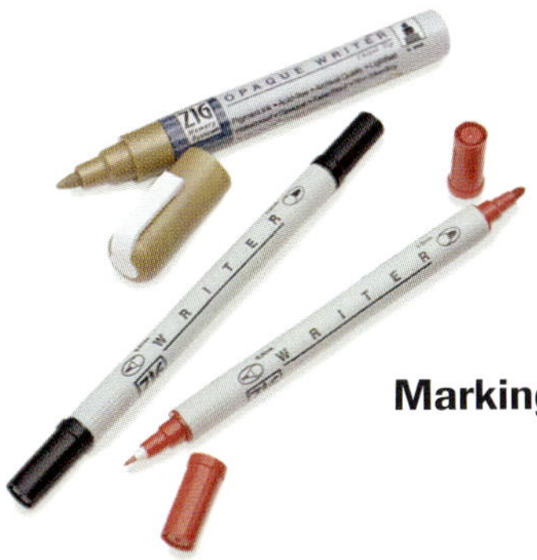

Marking Pens

Metal Embellishments

Metal Embellishments

Used to enhance scrapbook pages quickly, metal embellishments include mini frames, trims, charms, chains, and other items. When choosing embellishments consider the weight and placement of the items.

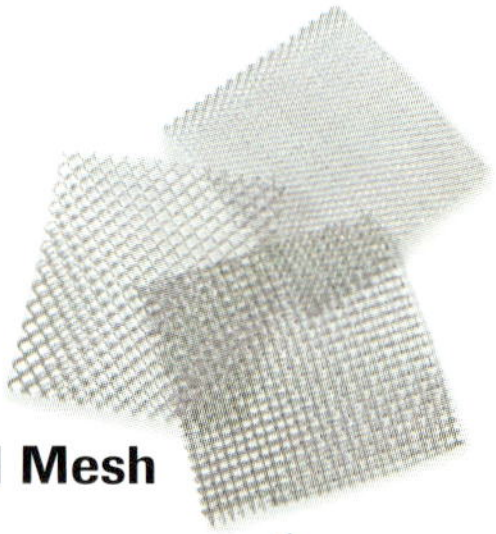

Metal Mesh

Metal Mesh

This mesh is similar to window screen and available in sheets of different designs and colors.

Paper Trimmer

Paper Trimmer

This is a gridded bed with a blade arm that cuts straight lines in paper. An essential scrapbooking tool, a paper trimmer makes cutting strips, squares, and rectangles quick and easy.

Photo Corners

Photo Corners

For years photo corners were used to hold photos in albums without placing adhesive directly on the photo back. Scrapbookers now have photo corners with intricate designs to complement the theme of the page.

Photo Markers

Photo Markers

These pastel markers give subtle color to black and white photos. The different tip widths allow for coloring in large or small areas.

Precut Papers

Precut Papers

Scrapbooking stores carry a selection of papers cut into squares and rectangles to make color-blocking and matting swift and simple. Purchase these papers in a bag or in a stack that is bound on one edge.

Protective Sleeves

Usually acid free, these plastic pockets come in sizes to fit scrapbooks. The sleeves protect pages from deteriorating elements.

Protective Sleeves

Rubber Stamps and Ink Pad

Transfer images of all sorts to paper using rubber stamps. The raised area on the stamp is pressed onto an ink pad and then pressed onto paper. Thousands of stamp designs are available, and ink pads come in every color, including metallics and blends.

Rubber Stamps and Ink Pad

Scissors

The type of scissors that works best for scrapbooking is sharp, short, and pointed, to enable you to make detail cuts on paper.

Scissors

Tags

Premade tags lend quick detail to scrapbooking pages and can be used as a background for journaling, stickers, labeling, or other embellishments. The tags shown here have metal edges. The punched hole allows for attachment using such items as fibers, brads, or eyelets.

Tags

Vanishing-Ink Pen

This marking pen has ink that fades, perfect for creating a temporary mark or guide.

Vanishing-Ink Pen

how to use your supplies

Photo Trimmer

Circle Cutter

Vanishing-Ink Pen, Ruler, and Stickers

Trimming Photos

A small version of a paper trimmer, a photo trimmer is a convenient tool with a flat gridded surface for measuring and a blade that makes straight cuts. Some models have a shield next to the blade to hold the photo in place when pressure is applied. Use this tool with caution and keep fingers away from the blade.

To use the trimmer, lift the blade arm up by the handle with one hand. With the other hand, position the photo on the gridded surface, using the lines for measurement. Press on the shield and carefully push the blade handle down until the length of the photo is cut.

Cutting Circles

Cut out perfect circles using a circle cutter, which has a sharp blade that follows the shape of the base. Most circle cutters are sold with a mat made specially for protecting the work surface. The cutter shown here comes with a thick square of glass.

To use the cutter determine the size of circle desired and adjust the blade to that size. Set a protective mat on the cutting surface. Place the paper to be cut on the protective mat. Position the cutter on the paper, apply pressure to the top handle, and move the blade arm around the circular center.

To make half circles, place the tool at the paper edge or cut a whole circle in half with scissors.

Aligning Alphabet Stickers

To draw a rule for perfect alignment, use a vanishing-ink pen. This temporary line helps when placing alphabet stickers and photos, journaling, and more.

First use a ruler and a vanishing-ink pen to draw a line where you want the letters. Use this line as a guide for positioning letters. The line will disappear soon.

Trimming Paper

A paper trimmer has a flat gridded surface for measuring and a blade that makes straight cuts. Available in several sizes and styles, these trimmers make cutting large sheets of paper a breeze. Some models have a shield next to the blade to hold the paper in place when pressure is applied. Use this tool with caution and keep fingers away from the blade.

To use the trimmer, lift the blade arm up by the handle with one hand. With the other hand, position the paper on the gridded surface, using the lines for measurement. Press on the shield and carefully push the blade handle down until the length of the paper is cut.

Paper Trimmer

Securing Brads

A great jazzy way to decorate with small accents of color and shape, these metal embellishments are supersimple to apply to scrapbook pages. Brads are available in round, square, and decorative shapes.

Use a pencil to mark brad placement. Punch a tiny hole at the mark to avoid bending the paper. From the front of the paper, insert the prongs through the hole, separate the prongs, and bend them outward from one another until flat against the back of the paper.

Brads

Handheld Eyelet Tool

Eyelet Tool, Mat, and Hammer

Decorating Chalk

Setting Eyelets

Eyelets are small metal embellishments that leave a hole in the center of the design once set. They hold papers together and serve as design elements. Eyelets are available in a wide assortment of shapes and colors, including metallic.

Two methods can be used for setting eyelets. For either method, use a pencil to mark the eyelet placement. Punch a tiny hole at the mark and insert the tube part of the eyelet into the hole from the front of the paper.

One method of securing the eyelet is to use a handheld tool, *above left*. Resembling a paper punch, the tool clamps the eyelet, spreading apart the small tube area of the eyelet to hold the paper between the front and back of it. When using this tool, hold it so the tooth (bump) is on the bottom. Insert the tooth into the tube part of the eyelet and squeeze closed. This technique limits the positioning of the eyelet, as it reaches only a short length from the edge of the paper.

The second method is to use an eyelet tool (small metal rod), a protective mat, and a hammer. Place the eyelet through the starter hole and turn, right side down, on the protective mat. Place the eyelet tool in the tube part of the eyelet and strike with a hammer until secure.

Chalking Paper

Available in scrapbooking stores, decorating chalk comes in a plethora of colors to create several effects. Scrapbooking chalk does not rub off or smudge after application. Use it to color elements, such as outlined letters, or to make a shadow around the edge of paper. This technique often is done using brown or black to give a vintage look.

Attaching Micro Beads

Micro beads are sand-size balls that give color, shine, and texture to many surfaces, including paper.

A quick way to create a strip of beaded texture is to place a strip of double-sided tape on paper and pour beads on the tape. Scrapbooking stores carry a selection of tape widths for this purpose. When pouring beads, place the paper in a shallow container to catch the excess.

Micro Beads

Using Adhesive Spacers

Adhesive spacers are sticky foam pads sold in dots, squares, and rolls that are tacky on both sides. They quickly attach an element to the background paper, raising it from the page. Spacers are available in a range of sizes and thicknesses.

To use the spacers remove one side of the backing paper and press onto the element to be attached. Remove the backing paper from the other side of the spacer and place the element where desired. Depending on the size of the element, you may want to use more than one spacer.

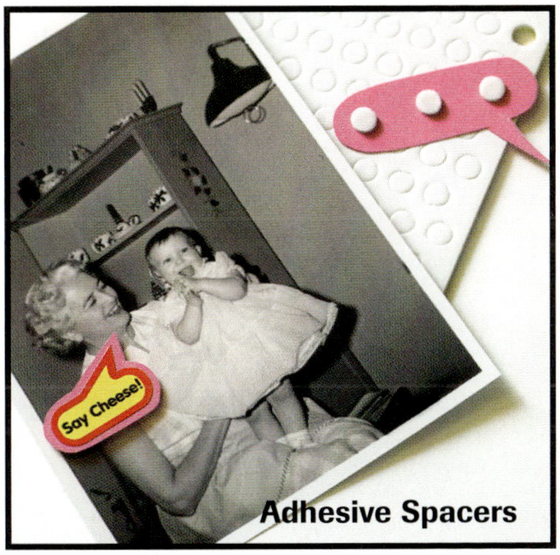

Adhesive Spacers

Using Templates

Templates (stencils) are plastic or cardboard sheets that have die-cut shapes used for patterns. Most templates have several shapes on one sheet.

To use a template lay it on the paper to which you wish to transfer the design. Using a pencil trace around the template. Use the drawn line as a guide for coloring, writing, and cutting.

Templates

Journaling

A quick way to ensure journaling in a straight line is to use the edge of a rectangle of heavy paper, such as card stock.

To use the straightedge, align the edge with the paper to be journaled. Use the edge of the card stock to guide writing. For letters with descenders (letter parts that fall below the guide line), write in descenders when all the journaling is complete. Replace the card stock when the edge becomes indented.

Straightedge Journaling

8 terrific tips!

1 Get organized

Scrapbooking progresses more smoothly when your photos are organized beforehand. Choose only the best photos to represent each event.

2 Set aside time

The most productive scrapbookers regularly set aside time to work on their albums. Whether late at night after the kids are in bed or a weekend evening spent cropping, schedule time for scrapbooking.

3 Do your prework

Break your scrapbooking into smaller tasks to do at opportune times. Perhaps make a bag of punched shapes while waiting to pick up a child from dance or cut paper strips while watching TV.

4 Have a goal for each page

Think about the main point of the page. What message are you trying to convey?

5 Copy pages you like

Whether an original sketch or an idea from a book or magazine, use these layouts as models for your pages.

6 Repeat, repeat, repeat

When you find a layout you like, repeat it on another scrapbook page later in your album using different colors and embellishments. If possible make the pages during one sitting for efficiency.

7 Shop with photos in hand

Select photos, put them in an envelope, and take them with you when shopping at the scrapbook store. Pick out papers and embellishments to coordinate with the photos, asking for assistance from the store staff if needed.

8 Make a theme album

Choose the same color scheme and embellishments for an entire album to create continuity in the album's look and feel. This works well for many types of themes, such as baby and wedding. It also saves time when selecting iter for each page.

10 timesaving actions

❶ Mix Print Paper and Card Stock

Use strips of card stock and print paper in varying widths to construct your layout in no time. Use premade strips or cut or tear your own. (See an example on *page 138.*)

❷ Use a Page Kit

A nicely designed page kit yields layouts in a flash. Choose a kit carefully; look for colors that coordinate with your photos. Often page kits contain enough materials to complete several pages. (See an example on *page 145.*)

❸ Use a Monochromatic Color Scheme

Planning appropriate colors for scrapbook pages is often difficult and time-consuming. One way to speed up the process is to use a monochromatic (one-color) theme. Choose a focus color; then choose coordinating card stock in at least three shades of that color—light, medium, and dark. (See an example on *pages 180–181.*)

❹ Mat with Premade Frames

Use premade frames to save work. The frames, often accompanied by matching embellishments, fill your pages and give a professional look instantly. Choose your frames carefully to match photos and papers. (See an example on *page 139.*)

❺ Color-Block the Background

Color-blocking is a simple technique in which blocks of solid or print card stock or papers are arranged to create a background or photo mat. Select three to four colors from your photos and choose papers to match. (See an example on *page 133.*)

6 Create a Title from Stickers

Use alphabet stickers to create a headline block, selecting stickers that complement the theme. Press them on card stock, leaving room for journaling if desired. Embellish the page with coordinating decorative stickers. (See an example on *page 182.*)

7 Rubber-Stamp the Background

Customize a layout by rubber-stamping randomly on the background paper. Use acid-free scrapbooking ink that coordinates with layout colors. To make embellishments, stamp on a piece of card stock and cut around the shapes for an economic alternative to stickers. (See an example on *pages 236–237.*)

8 Create a Large Vertical Headline

Divide your layout into imaginary thirds. Print or place your headline on a strip of card stock to cover the left third of the page. Fill the remainder of the page with evenly spaced photos. (See an example on *page 237.*)

9 Make Borders from Punches

Punches are available in a wide range of designs and sizes to create instant borders. Punch shapes from paper scraps and align them to make thrifty substitutes for purchased borders. (See an example on *pages 184–185.*)

10 Make a Single-Photo Layout

Choose a good photo and let it do most of the work. If the photo image is strong or enlarged, little embellishment is needed. (See an example on *page 186.*)

Heaven Sent
Anne Mae
June 5. 1987
5lbs 5½ oz.

Gather all those darling photos of your little angels and get ready to scrap cute-as-a-bug pages you'll treasure forever.

oh baby!

QUICK TIP

Use the edge of the photo mat to help align stickers.

splish splash

Make it playful using a purchased photo strip of rubber ducks to guide the color choices for paper and lettering. As a final touch apply whimsical character stickers on the page to look as though they are sitting or walking along the papers.

materials

- photo
- 12-inch square of turquoise textured card stock
- rubber ducky photo strip
- yellow print alphabet stickers
- white alphabet stickers
- print papers in turquoise and white, and yellow and white
- animated animal stickers
- paper cutter or crafts knife and metal ruler
- adhesive

Lettering aligns with left edge of photo for an organized appearance.

Two colors, turquoise and yellow, tie the page together.

Fun characters seem to make the baby in the photo smile.

A purchased photo strip emphasizes bath time even more clearly than the photo.

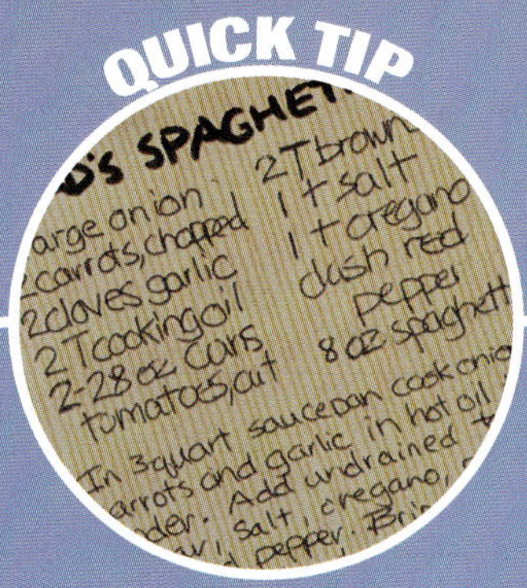

Draw journaling guides using a pen with disappearing ink.

dad's pasgetti

Make it interesting by combining a silly photo, a recipe, and paper strips. The messy nature of the spaghetti photo encourages the page to look somewhat haphazard while maintaining the focus on the baby in the photo.

Handwrite the recipe to personalize it.

Cut paper strips for spaghetti.

Use red plaid for borders that show without looking too bold.

Computer-generate a headline in large letters.

materials

- recipe
- photo
- 12-inch red subtle-print card stock
- papers in red plaid, black and white polka dot, yellow stripe, green print, and ivory
- pen with disappearing ink
- black marking pens in fine and medium widths
- computer and printer
- scissors
- paper cutter
- adhesive

QUICK TIP

Bring attention to the headline by adding a dimensional element.

simply beautiful

Make it monochromatic using three shades of one color. To texturize the page, overlay printed vellum, a length of fiber, headline and journal boxes, and a metal heart and frame. The size and placement of photos creates visual flow.

materials

- photos
- 12-inch square of dark pink card stock
- card stock scraps in medium and light pink
- 12-inch square of light pink printed vellum
- metal heart and small photo frame
- computer and printer
- paper trimmer
- thick white crafts glue
- adhesive

Tear pieces of vellum and layer on the page.

Print the headline and tear the edges.

Adhere a length of fiber along the right edge; tape on back.

li'l sister, big sister

Make it coordinated by mounting one large photo on solid card stock that coordinates with the background paper. Although you could emulate the look of striped background paper, purchase it that way and save yourself time.

Organize threaded buttons in rows and adhere with crafts glue.

Choose card stock to stand out from print background paper.

Print headline in three lines to fill space.

QUICK TIP

Use a long length of embroidery floss and a sewing needle to make threading buttons easy.

materials

- photos
- 12-inch square of partially striped paper
- 3 colors of coordinating card stock
- coordinating small-stripe paper
- coordinating buttons
- white embroidery floss
- sewing needle
- computer and printer
- paper trimmer
- thick white crafts glue
- adhesive

QUICK TIP

Thread textured yarn through a charm for a stunning accent.

materials

- photo
- 12-inch square of blue card stock
- 12-inch square of baby-print scrapbook paper
- light green card stock
- blue and pink textured yarn
- safety pin charm
- baby bracelet dimensional trim
- micro beads
- ¼-inch-wide double-sided tape
- computer and printer
- paper trimmer
- thick white crafts glue
- adhesive

first days

Make it sparkle by adding beads. Choose a premade dimensional baby bracelet (or make your own) and edge the journal box with strips of micro beads.

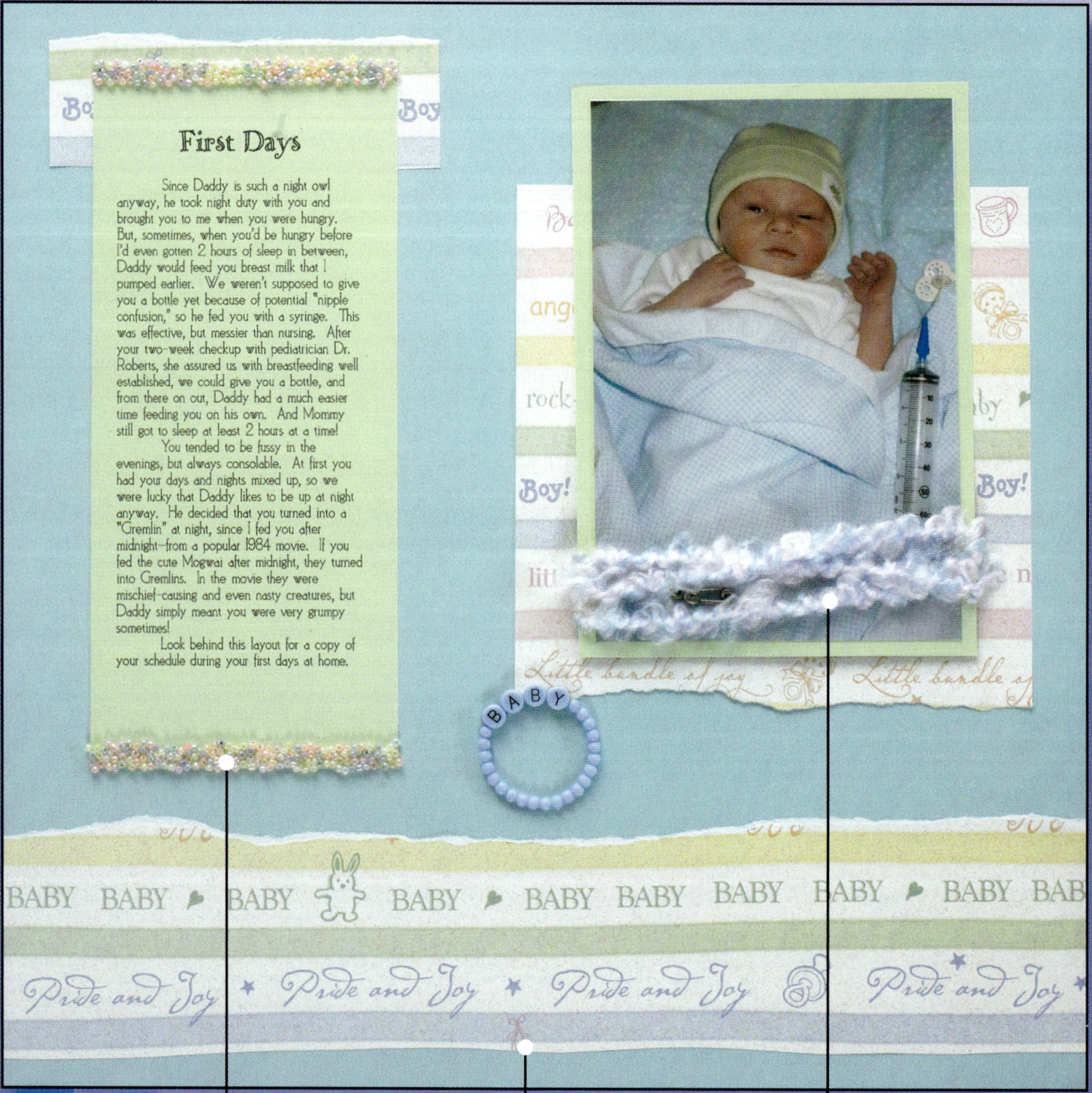

Place strips of double-sided tape at the top and bottom of the journal box and cover them with micro beads.

Trim one long edge irregularly and tear the other.

Wrap the photo with yarn threaded through a charm.

who's that baby?

Make it graphic using paper scraps to make a geometric design. Display precut glass and mirrors to carry out the theme and reflect a beautifully artistic image.

QUICK TIP

If you don't have the right color of paper on hand, use fabric.

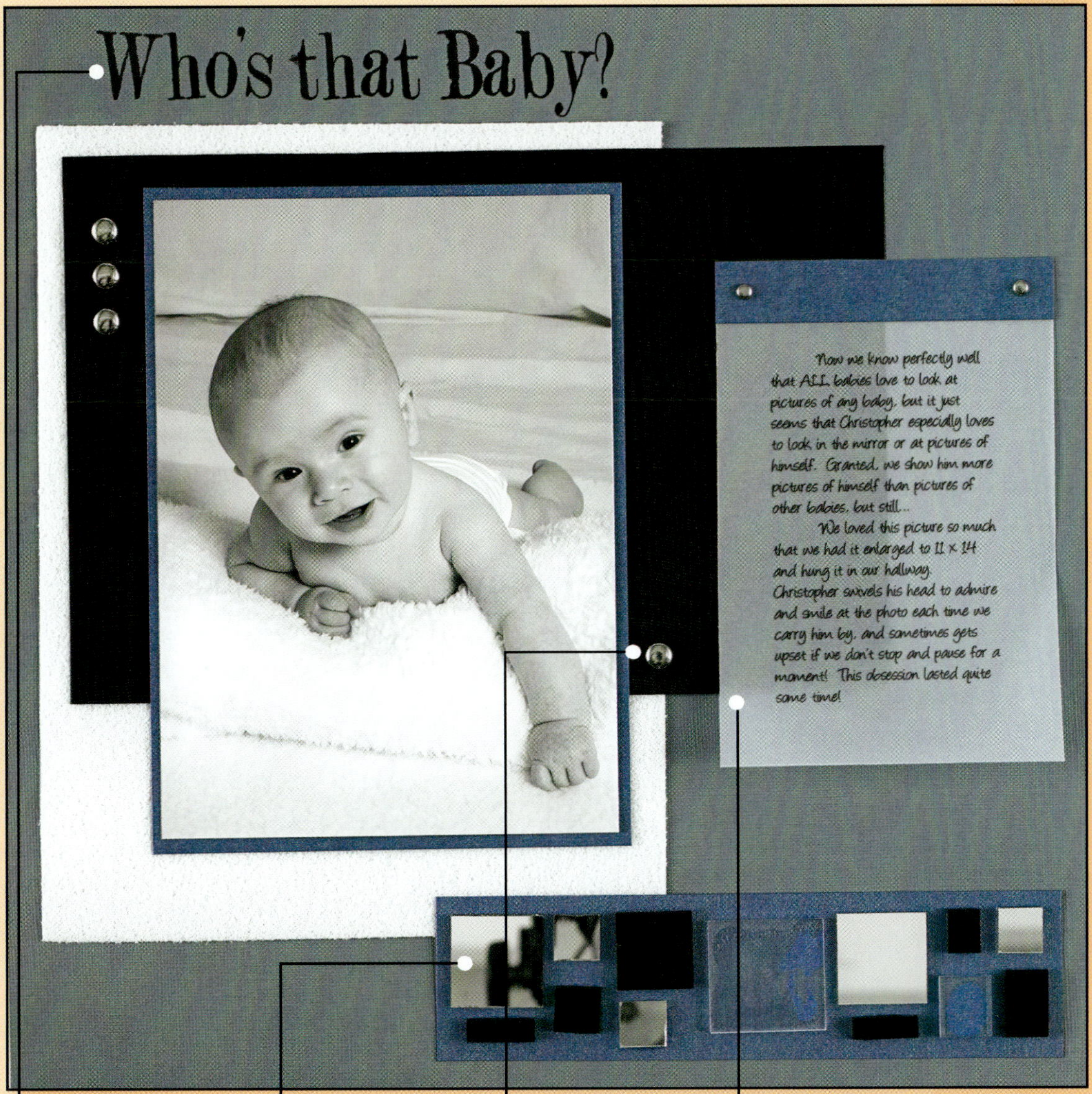

Print or stamp the headline on the background card stock.

Arrange and glue mirrors and glass on a rectangular piece of paper.

Dress up the page with brads.

Print journaling on vellum and top with a card stock strip.

materials

- photo
- 12-inch square of blue-gray card stock
- white fiber paper
- iridescent blue paper
- vellum
- black moiré fabric
- large and small silver brads
- small glass and mirror squares and rectangles
- computer and printer
- paper trimmer
- paper punch
- glass adhesive, such as Diamond Glaze glue
- adhesive

first swim

Make it easy by coordinating a geometric print background and photo matting paper. The paper's design enhances the page with instant detail while allowing the photos to remain the focal point. If you don't find papers like these but like the look, just use a

materials

- photos
- 12-inch square of geometric print card stock
- coordinating stripe paper for mat
- water-print paper
- white card stock
- white corrugated paper
- chalk in turquoise and green
- glass mosaic tiles in two sizes
- paper cutter
- scissors
- computer and printer
- double-sided tape
- adhesive

Use double-sided tape to hold mosaic tiles in place.

Allow the print in the paper to organize the page.

Choose an outline font to print on patterned scrapbook paper for the headline.

square punch to make the grid squares and a paper trimmer to make the horizontal rules for the photo mat. With just a little more effort you can create this geometric page. Add a few mosaic tiles to enhance the square look, and this page is a winner.

Mat a favorite photo as a focal point.

Rub chalk on raised areas of the corrugated strip and on the edges of the journal box.

Align photos vertically, leaving a small space between them.

QUICK TIP

Dress up a journal box with corrugated paper and chalk.

firsts

Make it artistic by framing an enlarged photo with premade art embellishments. These sweet-as-pie headlines, checked border strips, stars, flowers, bugs, and journal boxes are all provided on *pages 289* and *291*. You can cut and use the papers right from the

materials

- photo
- 12-inch square of purple scrapbook paper
- 12-inch square of light yellow-orange scrapbook paper
- 12-inch square of polka-dot paper
- color photocopy of art elements, pages 289 and 291
- marking pens in purple and blue
- scissors
- adhesive

see pages 289 and 291

Mount the silhouette on polka-dot paper.

Trim polka-dot paper in an irregular, straight-edge shape.

Cross the border strips at the corners.

book or, better yet, photocopy them so you can use the elements again and again. When trimming the art elements, leave a narrow black border to separate the pieces from the background. This helps to keep the page neat.

Trim checked strips to make square corners.

Position dots from the bug to the conversation bubble.

Write a comical blurb with a marker.

QUICK TIP

Salvage a photo with an undesirable background by cropping it and mounting it on paper.

Art in back of book!

see pages 289 and 291

QUICK TIP

Lightly rub sandpaper across blank paper surface to create a distressed look.

daddy's boy

Make it striking using three quality closeup photographs and simple embellishments. Choose papers that contrast with the photographs so your baby's face remains the focus of the page.

materials

- photos
- 12-inch squares of card stock in blue and dark red
- $10\frac{1}{2}$-inch square of blue typed-word print paper
- $11\frac{1}{2}\times2$-inch strip of blue and black plaid paper
- 2 brads
- gold buckle
- black alphabet stickers
- "daddy's boy" dimensional stickers
- fine sandpaper
- paper punch
- black fine-line permanent marking pen
- hot-glue gun and glue sticks
- adhesive

Create the look of hand-stitched lines using a marking pen.

Balance the red paper strip with a 2-inch-wide plaid paper strip.

Apply alphabet stickers in a wavy line.

Thread the paper strip through the buckle; secure buckle with hot glue.

anné mae

Make it heavenly using the papers on *pages 293* and *295.* Use the paper as it is or reduce or enlarge the elements to suit your needs. *Page 295* features alternate art to use or photocopy, including a journal box, strips of star paper, and star circles.

QUICK TIP

For a facing scrapbook page, copy the art using a mirror image.

Use the papers on pages 293 and 295 to create your page.

Select a photo with the baby's eyes looking up toward the angels.

Choose a banner from page 295 to record pertinent information.

Separate the painterly papers by mounting the top mat on solid blue paper.

materials

- photo
- papers or photocopies of paper on pages 293 and 295
- 8½×11-inch card stock
- deep blue paper
- copier or scanner
- crafts knife
- scissors
- marking pen
- adhesive

Art in back of book!

see pages 293 and 295

QUICK TIP

Combine stamping and punched letters for an interesting headline.

start in art

Make it meaningful with your child's artwork as the main ingredient of the page. Focus attention on the artwork by using a minimum of embellishments.

materials

- child's flat artwork
- 12-inch square of light blue card stock
- dark blue card stock
- art-theme border
- alphabet rubber stamp
- black ink pad
- alphabet punch
- paper cutter
- adhesive

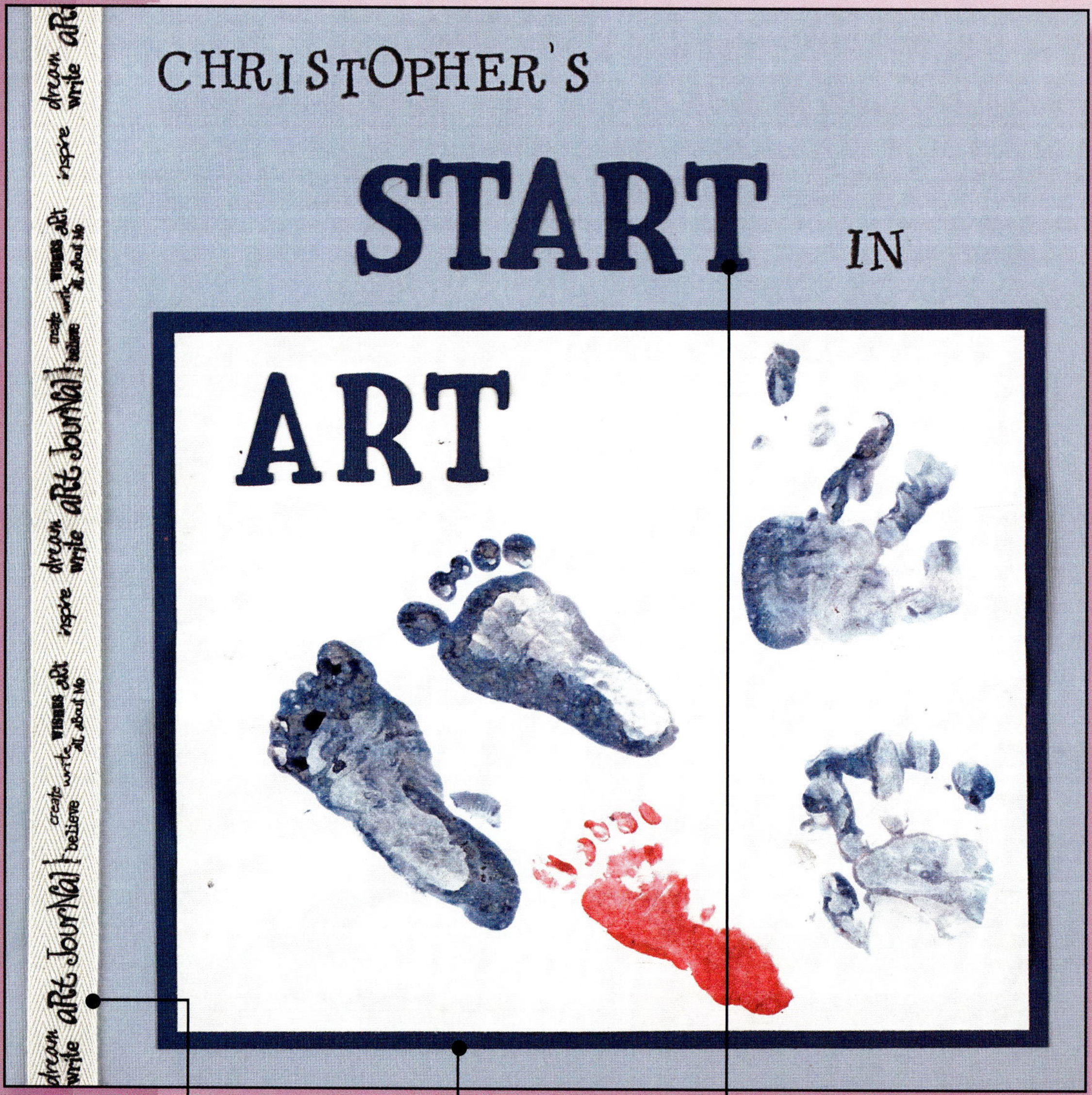

Place the border vertically on the page.

Mount the artwork on contrasting card stock.

Punch some of the headline letters from the contrasting card stock.

baby album

Make it adorable using only three decorative papers and ready-made stickers and other embellishments to create an entire booklet in just a few hours.

Crop photos in ovals to highlight the subject.

Limit the number of papers to three to lend continuity to the pages.

Use stickers to make journaling quick and easy.

Cut decorative papers in squares and strips for page accents.

QUICK TIP

Spotlight one photo per page.

materials

- photos
- 7¼×5½-inch pieces of white card stock
- pink print paper
- green print paper
- yellow card stock
- pink letters
- assorted stickers
- small vellum poem sticker
- large vellum poem sticker
- adhesive

They're busy, curious, fun-loving, and sweet—kids give us never-ending reasons to scrapbook.

love those kids

QUICK TIP

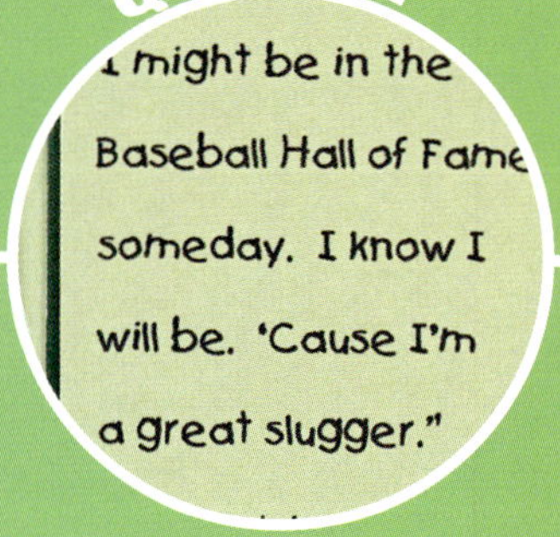

Use a quote to make journaling a breeze.

batter up

Make it fast using papers and premade embellishments that relate to the photos. Here striped paper imitates the look of the fence, and easy-mount tiles give the impression of a baseball diamond.

materials

- photos
- 12-inch square of light green card stock
- card stock in light and dark green
- striped gray scrapbook paper
- alphabet stickers
- square punch
- light green self-adhesive tiles
- paper trimmer
- computer and printer
- adhesive

Arrange self-adhesive tiles to form a large diamond shape.

Punch squares in a card stock strip; adhere alphabet stickers in the openings.

Print and mount a quote, leaving room for embellishments at the bottom.

texas princess

Make it balance by placing print paper strips above and below a row of mounted photos. Make the strips the same size, allowing room for the photos in the center. Cut the strips slightly smaller than the background paper width to leave a narrow border all around.

QUICK TIP

Draw circles on a tag with disappearing ink and use as guides for journaling.

Use a brad to hold each flower die-cut in place.

Print words on ribbon, using repositionable adhesive to hold ribbon to paper while printing from a computer.

Cut bands of card stock to top each mounted photo.

materials

- 4 photos, approximately $2\frac{1}{2}\times3\frac{1}{2}$ inches
- 12-inch square of light pink card stock
- 12-inch square of print scrapbook paper
- dark pink card stock
- acetate
- $\frac{1}{4}$-inch pink grosgrain ribbon
- $\frac{1}{8}$-inch pink satin ribbon
- ribbon holders
- metal-edge white tags in two sizes
- flower die-cuts in pink and white
- light green marker
- small paper punch
- brads
- paper trimmer
- repositionable adhesive
- adhesive

Apply meaningful word stickers to card stock and trim narrow borders.

cherish

Make it dramatic by enlarging a favorite photo to 8×10 inches for impact. Overlap it with a word-print paper turned so the words run sideways to prevent detracting from the photo.

materials

- 8×10-inch photo
- 12-inch square of burgundy card stock
- 10½×11¼-inch piece of pink card stock
- 11×8-inch piece of pink word-print paper
- card stock scraps in light and dark pink
- cream paper
- word stickers
- 3 round metal-edge tags
- assorted pink fibers and ribbons
- pink brads
- computer and printer
- scissors
- adhesive spacers, such as Pop Dots
- adhesive

Print a meaningful word and dictionary definition for the headline.

Use brads to attach the labels.

Glue card stock circles to tags and apply word stickers. Raise the top tag with adhesive spacers.

madison

Make it spectacular by pairing two coordinating big-print papers to frame a single photo. Divide the papers with a grosgrain ribbon and cut out two of the print images, such as the flowers, *below,* from the leftover paper.

QUICK TIP

Silhouette a couple of motifs from the top layer of paper and mount with adhesive spacers.

Cover the paper seam with ribbon.

Use different print papers on the top and bottom of the page.

Use a marking pen to write a brief description on the tag. Attach with double-sided tape.

materials

- photo
- two 12-inch squares of coordinating big-print papers
- yellow card stock
- 1-inch-wide yellow grosgrain ribbon
- 1×½-inch metal-edge white tag
- fine-line black marking pen
- paper trimmer
- scissors
- adhesive spacers, such as Pop Dots
- double-sided tape

QUICK TIP

Use stickers to embellish the page corners.

patriotic play

Make it simple by keeping trims to a minimum. The subtle patterns of the papers *below* create texture without overpowering the photos. To break up the background, use a contrasting paper, such as the red, on half of the page.

materials

- photos
- 12-inch square of blue polka-dot paper
- red check paper
- card stock in navy blue and white
- sticker border and corners
- small brads
- computer and printer
- small paper punch
- star punch
- paper cutter
- adhesive

Use theme-related stickers to embellish the page corners.

Poke small brads through paper layers to secure them and highlight corner details.

Punch shapes from card stock to fill void areas on journal blocks.

nice guy

Make it textured by wrinkling and tearing the papers. To create the look of leather, wrinkle card stock. To distress it further, tear a hole in it and turn back the edges around the hole. Tear a photo frame from red card stock, then roll back the edges of the opening.

QUICK TIP

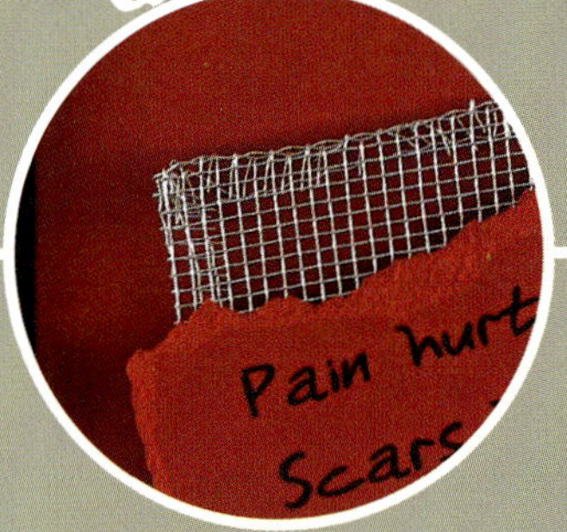

To make the page shine, fold under the edges of a piece of metal mesh and use it to back journaling.

Scrunch and smooth black card stock to resemble leather.

Fold back the edges of a torn hole and place mesh behind opening.

Use brads to hold torn journaling box in place.

materials

- photo
- 12-inch square and scraps of red card stock
- 12×5-inch piece of black card stock
- metal mesh
- eyelet-trim leather band
- small silver brads
- computer and printer
- paper punch
- scissors
- adhesive

QUICK TIP

Apply a shadow option to a headline font for increased impact.

fudge mystery

Make it checked by using squares of color. To make a checked background appearance, cut two squares from a color that contrasts with the background. Place them in opposite corners. Continue the square concept with small square paper accents and sharp square crops.

materials

- photos
- 12-inch square of medium blue card stock
- card stock in royal blue, medium blue, white, and red
- blue chalk
- red eyelets and eyelet tool
- paper trimmer
- adhesive

Use a computer to print journaling on a light color of card stock.

Attach programlike journaling with eyelets.

Overlap two small squares to give the headline intrigue.

two home runs

Make it personalized using easy personalization techniques. Use the baseball art provided on *pages 297* and *299*. Write a name on the ball using a marking pen. To make the headline, cut out the appropriate letters and adhere them in a row at the bottom of the page.

Use marking pen to personalize the baseball.

Run the stripe to the edge of the page.

Glue letters side by side to form headline.

QUICK TIP

Silhouette the desired shape to remove unwanted background.

materials

- photo
- 12-inch square of green scrapbook paper
- paper to back silhouette if needed
- blue card stock
- color photocopy of baseball art and letters, pages 297 and 299
- marking pens in black and 2 colors to coordinate with photo; scissors
- paper trimmer
- adhesive

Art in back of book!

see pages 297 and 299

sep rams

Make it themed by using strips of paper with a theme design to coordinate with the photos. Create a quick and easy scoreboard and headline using the ready-to-color art on *pages 297* and *299*. For the scoreboard, color in desired words with neon markers and fill in the

materials

- photos
- two 12-inch squares of yellow card stock
- navy blue card stock
- color photocopy of basketball, letter, and scoreboard art, pages 297 and 299
- paper trimmer
- scissors
- nonbleeding bright neon markers
- black marker
- markers in team colors
- adhesive tabs

see page 297

Silhouette enlargements for greater impact.

Use adhesive tabs to hold elements in place.

Overlap photos where there is a void in the background photo.

rest with black. For the headline and jersey number, use the main team hue to color around each letter. Arrange the letters side by side when connecting for a word.

Use a paper trimmer to cut strips quickly and accurately.

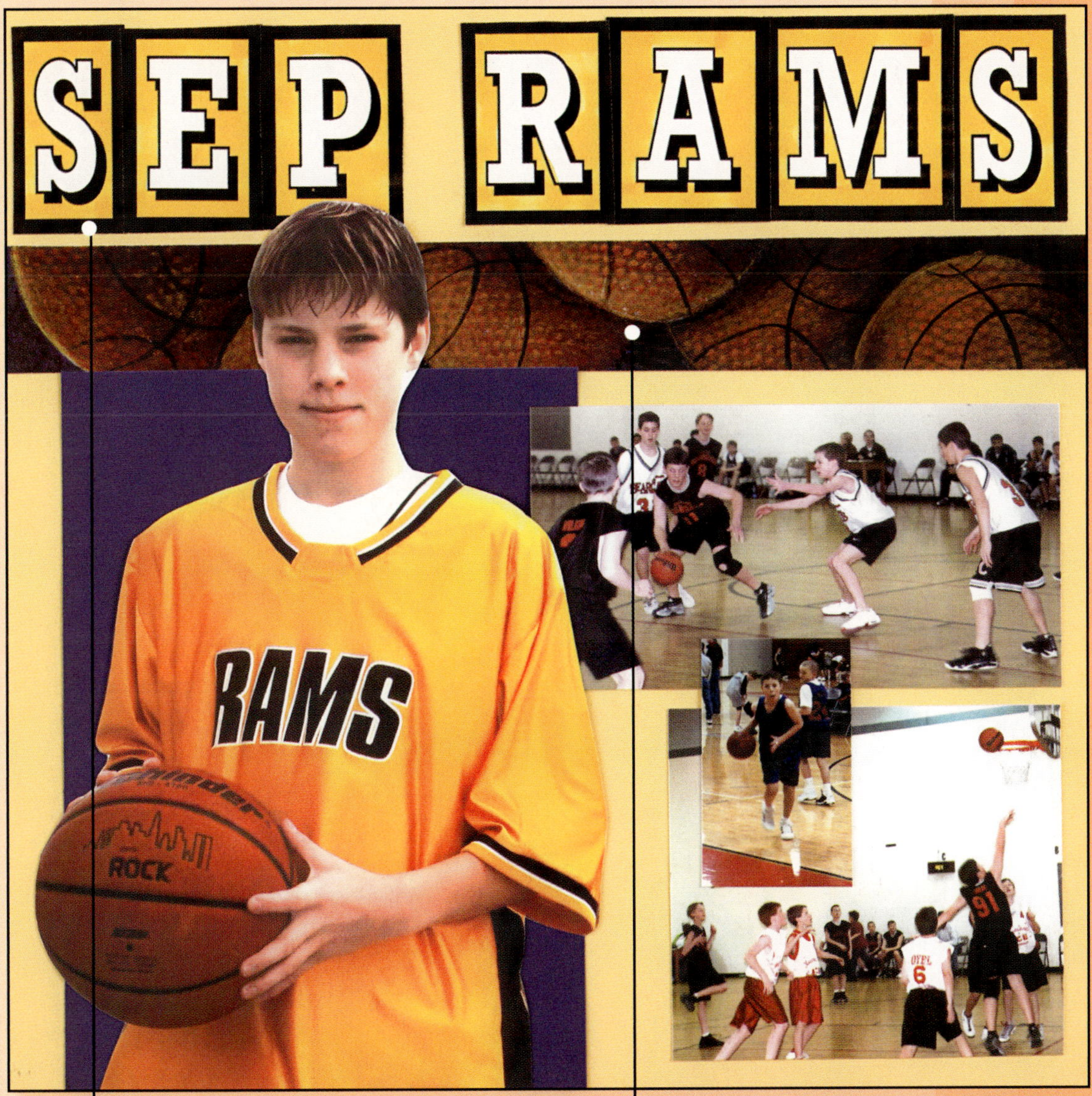

Enlarge the letters from page 297, cut out, and color with your team colors.

Enlarge the basketball border 115 percent to span a 12-inch page.

see page 297

QUICK TIP

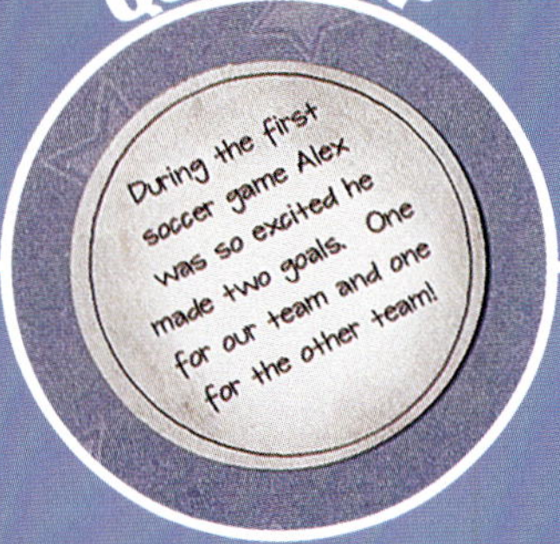

Place journaling in a soccer ball die-cut.

materials

- photos
- blue star pattern paper
- card stock in black and white
- die-cut letters
- mini soccer stickers
- goal sticker
- adhesive

soccer

Make it subtle using backgrounds that do not overpower photos. This blue-on-blue star paper backs people-packed photos with soft texture. Mat photos with black to pop and use varying-size crops for interest and to help the eye travel around the page.

Mount a vellum sticker on white card stock for emphasis.

Use black mats to separate photos from background.

Place soccer stickers on each letter to reinforce the theme.

Choose a subtle print that does not distract from the photos.

josh

Make it musical using purchased die-cuts to create the treble clef and wavy lines in the background. To achieve an embossed look, use the same color die-cuts as the background paper. Highlight the die-cuts by rubbing on silver tint to give them more definition.

Mat on silver for a classy frame on each photo.

Apply silver rub-on tint to cutouts to highlight.

Overlap an older black and white photo with a current color photo.

Handwrite white journaling for a striking accent on black.

QUICK TIP

Keep the photos as large as possible by extending them to the edge of the page.

materials

- photos
- 8½×11-inch piece of black paper
- paper cutter
- silver paper
- die-cuts of musical elements
- silver rub-on tint
- white opaque marker
- adhesive

sand volleyball

Make it picturesque using papers of natural textures, such as grass and sand. Before applying the sand-print paper on the grass-paper background, tear the edges of two sheets to make similar-size squares, then glue in place. Tuck some photos behind

materials

- photos
- 12-inch squares of grass-print paper
- sand-print paper
- wire mesh
- string
- scissors
- silver diamond dust paper
- self-sealing clear pocket
- die-cut letters
- volleyball stickers
- journaling volleyball
- adhesive

Real wire mesh creates the appearance of a volleyball net.

Use scraps of sand-print paper to make the headline.

A round die-cut works perfectly for journaling.

the netting. Place volleyball stickers strategically to pack the page with action. Stretch pieces of wire mesh across each page and tack them in place. Make the poles using silver diamond dust paper. Add pieces of string so the net appears to be tied to the poles.

QUICK TIP

Place volleyball stickers on a couple of photos to appear as balls in motion.

Place volleyball stickers strategically on photos to reinforce the theme.

Embellish the poles with string ties for a realistic look.

all-american

Make it newsworthy with newspaper clippings posted on a pseudo cork bulletin board. To make the thin cork stand out from the baseball-paper background, mount it on red and blue papers or

materials

- photos
- 12-inch square of sports-related paper
- four 12-inch squares of paper
- two 8½×11-inch pieces of thin corkboard (available in scrapbook stores and home improvement centers)
- photo mat
- sports appliqués (available in fabric and discount stores)
- star stickers
- paper cutter or crafts knife
- computer and printer
- newspaper clippings
- adhesive

Use a computer to print type.

Cover unrelated newspaper articles with pieces of cork.

Crop newspaper clippings to include in your pages.

papers in school colors. Finish off the page with vertical and horizontal type, photos, star stickers, and sports-theme emblems from a fabric store.

QUICK TIP

Dot the "i" with a sticker.

Place star stickers across both pages to link them.

Include stitched appliqués to reinforce the theme.

Use cork for texture and to act as a bulletin board, ready for displaying.

dance

Make it dimensional using pleated paper and ribbon. To make the tutu, enlarge and trace the pattern on *page 58.* Cut the printed paper in half and fold the pieces back and forth to create irregular pleats. Tape across the top back to hold pleats in place. Use the pattern to

materials

- photos
- tracing paper and pencil
- enlarged photocopy of pattern on page 58
- scissors
- two 12-inch squares of background paper
- 12-inch square of coordinating patterned paper
- two 12-inch squares of card stock
- coordinating paper scraps for shoes and photo mats
- tape; transfer paper
- ½-inch-wide ribbon and ⅛-inch-wide satin ribbon
- white paper
- scallop-edge decorative scissors
- black fine-line permanent marking pen
- floral photo corners
- bouquet sticker
- adhesive

Cut photos using an oval template.

Overlay the ovals with floral stickers.

Use scallop-edge scissors to cut a dainty border around photos.

Use transfer paper to transfer the headline to the upper left corner.

QUICK TIP

Write journaling around a shape to create interest.

cut out the tutu, legs, and shoes. Affix the pieces to the background papers, adding ribbon and paper embellishments as shown. If a flat embellishment is preferred, cut the bow pieces instead of tying them. Use the Dance pattern on *page 58* as a guide for lettering.

Draw dotted lines to add detail and definition to shapes.

Folded paper creates dimension for the tutu.

Use photo corner stickers as decorative accents.

A large silhouette balances the two photos opposite.

dance continued

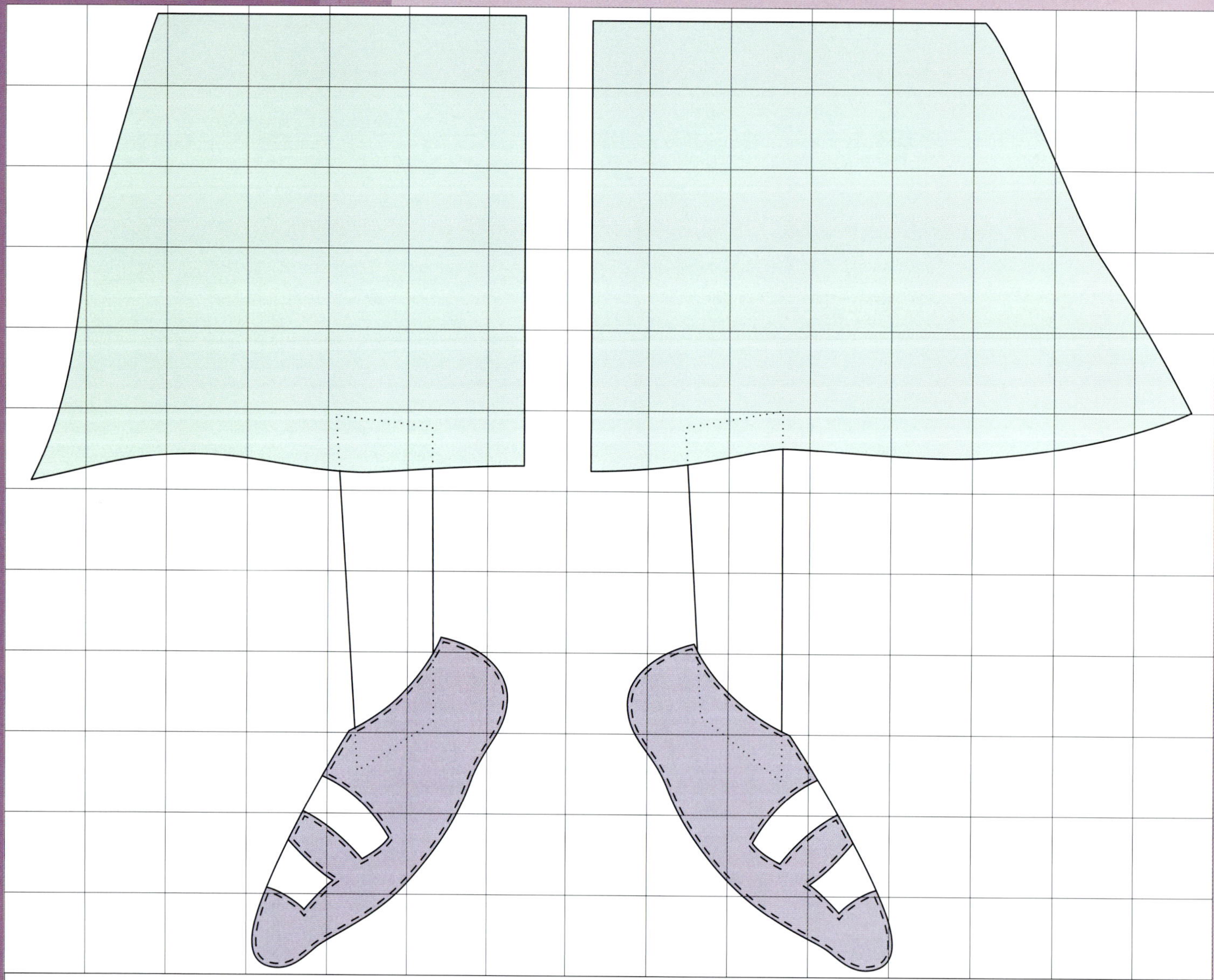

DANCER PATTERNS

1 SQUARE = 1 INCH

HEADLINE PATTERN

ben

Make it overlap by using three similar photos in graduated sizes. Place the photos on the page to overlap in a diagonal configuration. Counterbalance the photos by placing die-cuts that match the theme in the open corners.

QUICK TIP

Use a stencil and a white opaque marking pen to outline letters for a short headline.

Run the die-cuts off the page and trim even with page edge.

Use a plate to draw guidelines for curved lettering.

Trim letters to allow the white pen outline to show.

materials

- 3 photos in graduated sizes
- 12-inch square of dark blue card stock
- gold subtle-print paper
- leaf die-cuts or color photocopies of leaves
- alphabet stencil
- scissors
- paper trimmer
- white opaque marking pen
- adhesive

american girl camp

Make it quick by using precut shapes and die-cut embellishments. Place card stock triangles in the page corners to replicate the quiltlike die-cut designs.

QUICK TIP

Highlight the headline with a coordinating button tied with embroidery floss.

materials

- photos
- 12-inch square of white card stock
- card stock in dark blue, dark red, and white
- precut dark red triangles
- quilt-theme die-cuts
- red heart button
- blue embroidery floss
- sewing needle
- computer and printer
- paper trimmer
- adhesive

Place card stock triangles in the page corners.

Double-mat your favorite photo.

When necessary mount die-cuts on card stock so they stand out from the background.

Print the headline and journaling in one block for efficiency.

drummer girl

Make it organized by picking gray color-block background paper to lend order to the layout. Use the sections to arrange the components, overlapping the sections if desired, such as was done with the journal box on the lower left of the page.

Use a computer to print a quick headline.

Double-mat one photo to be the central focus of the page.

Align two photos of the same size.

Use a quote that relates to the theme.

materials

- photos
- 12-inch square of gray color-block card stock
- card stock in black, gray, and white
- computer and printer
- paper cutter
- adhesive

QUICK TIP

Use matching brads to attach the vellum headline.

materials

- photos
- 12-inch square of light teal card stock
- dark teal card stock
- 2 yellow-print papers
- vellum
- small teal brads
- computer and printer
- paper trimmer
- small paper punch
- black fine-line permanent marking pen
- adhesive

new friends

Make it mix and match by combining solid and two print papers. Balance the page by distributing the color and extending some shapes to the page edge. Print the headline and journaling on vellum to tell the story while allowing the background to show through.

Print photos with a white border when possible to save on mounting time and paper expenses.

Use a permanent black marking pen to draw a quick border.

Print type on vellum to allow the background to show through.

girly girl

Make it fun by combining premade items. Incorporate adhesive mesh, brads, button motifs strung on yarn, and a slide mount—all to coordinate with your papers. Use the button patterns on *page 276* to make bright buttons to parade across the page.

Use a slide mount for personalization.

Accent mesh strips using brads.

Use patterns on page 276 to make buttons from card stock.

Arrange punched letters in a random, tipped fashion.

QUICK TIP

Punch holes in die-cuts and thread with yarn, string, narrow ribbon, or embroidery floss.

materials

- photo; 12-inch square of black card stock
- 12-inch square of button-print paper
- card stock in bright colors; yellow yarn
- photocopy of button patterns, page 276
- adhesive yellow mesh, such as Magic Mesh
- brads; paper punch
- pink slide mount
- alphabet punches
- tracing paper; pencil
- paper trimmer
- black marking pen
- scissors; adhesive
- adhesive spacers

Patterns in back of book

see page 276

QUICK TIP

Place stickers where papers overlap to help hold papers in place.

best friends

Make it anchored by printing the headline on light-color background paper. To embellish the page place stickers and paper triangles in an artistic arrangement around the photo.

materials

- photo
- 12-inch square of pink card stock
- $11\frac{1}{2}$-inch square of lavender textured card stock
- $8\frac{1}{2} \times 11$-inch piece of pink parchment paper
- metallic gold paper
- heart vellum stickers
- scissors
- computer and printer
- adhesive

Balance the photo with careful sticker placement.

Layer papers to make a quick background.

Crop the photo to leave a white border, if possible.

Use scissors to cut triangles from metallic gold paper.

blocks

Make it special by using coordinating buttons for accents. For detail tie them with embroidery floss or mount them on small card stock squares.

QUICK TIP

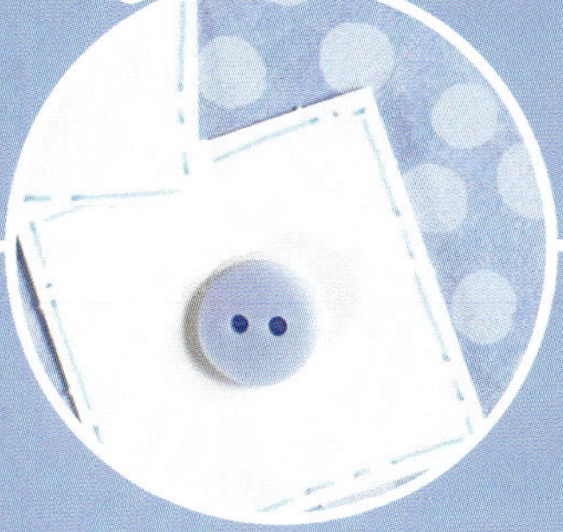

Create an instant border around a paper shape by drawing a broken line.

Use a word sticker below the boxes.

Use a template to make letters for the headline.

Print journaling in a color to coordinate with the page.

Accent copy blocks with eyelets.

materials

- photos
- 12-inch square of blue polka-dot paper
- coordinating stripe paper
- white card stock
- alphabet template
- blue buttons
- embroidery floss
- sewing needle
- stickers in rickrack and phrase motifs
- vellum
- eyelets
- eyelet tool
- computer and printer
- paper trimmer
- scissors
- adhesive
- thick white crafts glue

marching band

Make it bright using colored paper bands, bold rickrack, and contrasting embroidered letters. To make the M and B stand out, cut circles from contrasting paper and place behind the letters. Run rickrack in two rows across the top of both pages to give them

Use stitched appliqués horizontally and vertically for a striking headline.

Use a musical note stamp to emphasize the band theme.

Follow a mat shape with journaling to keep the page neat.

Place colored circles under letters to lead your eye.

materials

- photos
- two 12-inch squares of white card stock
- 6 accent papers in bright colors
- white paper
- rainbow-color rickrack
- musical note stamp
- gold stamp pad
- scissors
- circle cutter
- paper cutter
- stitched appliqué letters (available in the notion section of fabric and discount stores)
- line stickers
- floral buttons
- black fine-line marking pen
- adhesive
- crafts glue

QUICK TIP

Keep the writing organized by following the photo shapes.

the appearance of a unit. Stamp musical notes trailing from the left page to the right. Neatly silhouette some photos for interest. Write the journaling around the photos or in a wavy fashion to add to the playfulness of the spread.

Glue rickrack across the top of both pages to link them.

Snip shanks from buttons and glue the buttons in place using crafts glue.

Repeat circular shapes throughout the peppy layout.

QUICK TIP

Use different focus depths to bring interest to the page.

abby

Make it endearing using four basic shapes (rectangles, triangles, squares, and a tulip) and two colors (pink and green) for a graphic presentation.

materials

- photos
- 12-inch square of plaid background paper
- green paper
- tulip journal box and floral letters software
- scissors
- adhesive

Arrange letters vertically to provide an organized border for the page.

Place plaid paper squares on point for quiltlike quaintness behind the lettering.

Use a flower-shape journal box for a feminine touch.

Choose a background paper that brings out the color in the photo.

swing choir

Make it two-tone using pink papers that create a soft background for this special occasion. To add weight to the bottom, a coordinating paper was cut in half and glued horizontally across the page.

A subtle change in papers anchors the page.

materials

- photos
- 12-inch square of striped card stock
- 12-inch square of coordinating checked paper
- clear gel glue
- fine blue glitter marking pen
- scissors
- adhesive

Draw a freehand musical staff and draw glue and glitter notes.

Use gel glue and glitter to write a sparkling headline.

Silhouette a photo to draw attention to it.

2×2 twins turn 2

Make it celebratory with cake and candle cutouts. To get started enlarge the patterns *below* 200 percent on a photocopier. Trace and cut out the shapes. Trace around the shapes on the desired colors of card stock. Cut out shapes as well as a white X. Highlight the

materials

- photos
- tracing paper and pencil
- straight and decorative-edge scissors
- 12-inch square of turquoise polka-dot paper
- white card stock
- colored papers in green, purple, orange, and yellow
- yellow acrylic paint
- paintbrush
- yellow tube-style paint
- striped paper
- adhesive

CAKE, CANDLES, AND NUMBERS PATTERNS 1 SQUARE = 1 INCH

QUICK TIP

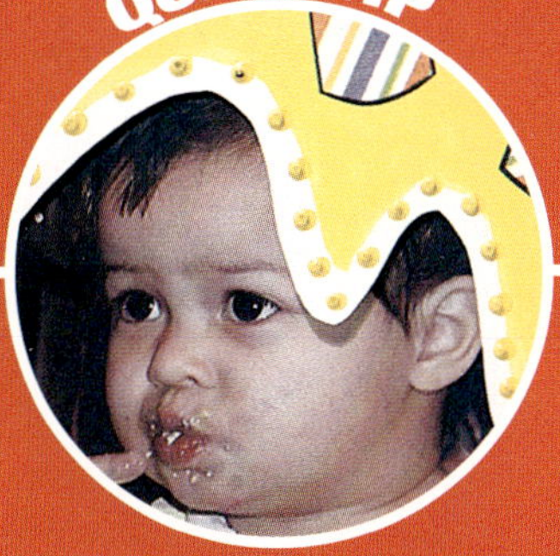

Create highlights using dots of acrylic paint.

frosting using paint. To make dots, dip the paintbrush handle tip into yellow paint and dot at the edge of the yellow paper. Make even dots around the edges of the frosting, redipping the paintbrush as needed.

Choose a background paper with a subtle confettilike design so as not to overpower the photos.

Paper strips cut with pinking shears add color and movement to the background.

Set the stage for a celebration with birthday cake photo mats.

scout pride

Make it authentic using a purchased club scarf in the background. Decide on the placement of the scarf and glue it to the paper, folding the raw edges to the back. Tape the edges in place. Create the look of a ribbon by cutting a wide strip with one end pointed.

materials

- photos and photocopy of certificate
- two 12-inch squares of white scrapbook paper
- cub Scout scarf
- tape
- papers in white, red, yellow-orange, and navy
- scissors and pinking shears
- crafts knife
- star stickers in gold and red
- red alphabet stickers
- adhesive

Use a fabric scarf to create a graphic background.

Use scarf scraps for bold accents..

Layer mats to unite the page colors.

Use paper strips and sticker letters and stars to complete the ribbon. Arrange the photos on the page, matting when necessary to allow them to stand out from the scarf background. Silhouette interesting shapes to avoid a totally blocky look.

QUICK TIP

Separate similar colors by adding a paper shadow behind the top color.

Use pinking shears to create decorative paper edges.

Silhouette photos to draw attention and balance page layout.

QUICK TIP

Draw a speech bubble on card stock and trim for a personal remark.

can I have a cow?

Make it spotted by tearing pieces of mulberry paper to create an animal skin look for the background. Brown mulberry paper is used here to resemble a cow's coat, but choose any color and tear it into spot shapes or stripes to depict the appropriate animal fur.

materials

- photos
- two 12-inch squares of white card stock
- brown mulberry paper
- $8\frac{1}{2}\times11$-inch paper to coordinate with photos
- blue card stock
- fine- and medium-tip black marking pens
- scissors
- paper trimmer
- adhesive

Place some of the photos to extend beyond the $8\frac{1}{2}\times11$-inch paper.

Choose a contrasting paper to separate the photos from the background.

Cut a speech bubble from white card stock and write a comment with a marking pen.

my baby

Make it storylike by writing a headline with an opaque marking pen and printing an in-depth journal box. These components, combined with a large and a small photo, are all you need for a successful page.

QUICK TIP

Dress up photo corners by trimming with a pair of decorative-edge corner scissors.

Print journaling to wrap around a circular photo.

Choose a color of opaque marker that shows up on the background.

Crop the small photo into a circle, silhouetting a detail to extend onto the mat.

materials

- photos
- 12-inch square of scrapbook paper
- coordinating solid-color card stock
- subtle-print scrapbook paper for journal box
- opaque marking pen
- circle cutter
- scissors
- paper trimmer
- decorative-edge corner scissors
- computer and printer
- adhesive

QUICK TIP

Crop favorite shots of each child, enlarging them if necessary.

peas in a pod

Make it creative using the decorative papers on *pages 301–309.* For a 12-inch-square page, enlarge the pea paper, plaid paper, and vine borders at 111 percent on a photocopier. Cut strips from papers in the desired widths to cover the background.

materials

- photos
- papers or photocopies of papers on pages 301–309
- 12-inch square of card stock
- scissors
- crafts knife
- colored pencils
- green marking pen
- adhesive

Copy and trim the art elements from pages 301–309.

To make the photos appear as one, color around the edges with colored pencil, the same color or darker.

Layer papers starting with the pea-dotted background, then layer the plaid and vine borders, headline banner, pea pod, journaling box, and decorative circle.

Art in back of book!

see page 301–309

emma and grandma

Make it resemble nature with a handmade landscape. Glue lavender tissue on the top portion of the ocher-color paper. Cut corn and leaves from tan and green paper strips and glue them in place. For flowers, fringe circles and add punched paper centers.

QUICK TIP

Glue on paper flowers last to overlap the photo and journaling.

Lightweight tissuelike paper simulates the fall foliage in the photo.

Cut circles with scallop-edge scissors and fringe them to make small blooms.

Colors in the photo are replicated on the scrapbook page.

Contrasting paper mats separate the photo from the background.

materials

- photo
- 8½×11-inch piece of ocher-color card stock
- lightweight tissue or rice paper, such as mulberry paper, in lavender, tan, and green
- papers to frame the photo
- papers for flowers, such as lavender, peach, yellow, and gold
- paper cutter
- spray adhesive
- scallop-edge decorative scissors and straight scissors
- paper punch
- marking pen
- adhesive

student driver

Make it silly by packing the page with meaningful photos that tell the story. Rather than searching for perfect art elements, photograph your own embellishments, such as road signs and a student driver sign to use for the headline. Use grass paper, gray, and blue to form

materials

- photos
- two 8½×11-inch pieces of blue card stock
- black paper
- grass-pattern paper
- solid-color papers in gray, yellow, brown, and white
- crafts knife
- black marking pen
- adhesive

Use a black permanent marking pen to add journaling to your photos.

Cut conversation bubbles and arrow shapes from white paper to use as backgrounds for personalized journaling.

Simple narrow black borders work well in this busy format.

a wavy yet uniform background. Have fun with the rest of the elements, tipping the photos and road signs to emphasize the fun. Write journaling directly on the photos or use speech bubbles cut from white paper. Outline the bubbles in black to stand out.

A silhouetted truck photo, tilted, with white marking pen lines creates animation. ■

Trim road sign photos and adhere to posts made from brown paper. ■

QUICK TIP

Use a closeup photograph of a vehicle sticker for the headline.

QUICK TIP

Turn square eyelets on point to make them appear as diamonds.

african tales

Make it quick using paper strips—just one sheet of card stock yields several. These make great page borders and are spectacular when accented with tiny paper rectangles and square eyelets.

materials

- photos
- 12-inch square of dark brown card stock
- card stock in white, red, and yellow
- square black eyelets
- eyelet tool
- branch rubber stamp
- dark red ink
- computer and printer
- paper trimmer
- adhesive

Silhouette an image from your photos.

Accent the journal box with a stamped image.

Print journaling so it wraps around a photo.

it's a teen thing

Make it clever with an interesting headline and minimal embellishments on the rest of the page. Here alphabet bottle cap die-cuts are used to spell the words. Raise a few of the die-cuts with adhesive spacers.

QUICK TIP

Cover the words of an old dog tag using alphabet stickers.

Raise some of the letters with adhesive spacers.

Cut out a circle using decorative-edge scissors to resemble a bottle cap.

Use a square tag to frame a photo and hang from chain.

materials

- photos
- 12-inch square of black card stock
- card stock in red and light green
- dog tags
- square tag
- ball chain
- alphabet bottle cap die-cuts
- square silver brad
- green marker
- paper trimmer
- small paper punch
- decorative-edge scissors
- adhesive spacers, such as Pop Dots
- adhesive

Add buttons to dress up a plain computer font.

our kids

Make it stitched using simple embroidery. Before stitching, mark (but do not cut) photo cutout areas. To make flowers, use a sharp needle and ribbon to make a French knot (see diagrams, *below left*) for each flower center. Surround each center with five lazy daisy petals.

materials

- photos
- 12-inch square of background card stock
- coordinating $8\frac{1}{2}\times11$-inch papers
- $\frac{1}{8}$-inch-wide embroidery ribbon and needle (available at fabric and crafts stores)
- flat buttons
- thick white crafts glue
- computer and printer
- adhesive

Combine lazy daisies and French knots to make dimensional ribbon flowers.

Use a crafts knife to cut out areas for photos.

Use running stitches to border photo cutouts.

Carry the yellow accent to the outer edge with narrow strips.

cotton candy days

Make it understated by mixing large photos and minimal embellishment. Here four photos nearly fill the page, leaving just enough room for a stamped headline and cotton candy accents.

QUICK TIP

For a polished look, glue baby rickrack along a seam where two papers meet.

materials

- photos
- 12×4-inch piece of lime green card stock
- 12×9-inch piece of pink polka-dot paper
- cardstock in pink, white, and lime green
- scrap of pink striped paper
- white baby rickrack
- large pink pom-pom
- pink flocking, such as Fun Flock
- alphabet stamps
- pink ink pad
- scissors
- paper trimmer
- adhesive
- thick white crafts glue

Dot green paper with crafts glue and sprinkle with flocking.

Cut a pom-pom in half to make cotton candy. Roll a 1×2-inch strip of paper for the handle.

Overlap the top paper strip 1 inch, gluing rickrack to secure the papers.

Preserve family remembrances with pages devoted to all the relatives dear to your heart.

all about family

QUICK TIP

Check the positioning of journaling on white paper before printing on acetate.

rough and tough

Make it see-through by printing the headline and journaling on acetate. This allows you to use different fonts and sizes of type and lets the background show through.

materials

- photo
- 12-inch square of light blue card stock
- 8½×11-inch sheet of acetate
- lightweight cardboard
- white paper tag and light blue envelope
- metal mesh
- washers
- brads
- alphabet stickers
- blue button
- swirl paper clip
- fibers in blue and brown
- scissors
- small paper punch
- computer and printer
- paper trimmer
- adhesive

Use a brad to attach each washer. Embellish the brad with an alphabet sticker.

Plan the headline to fall to the right of center and the journaling to wrap the photo.

Cut mesh rectangles and fold under the frayed edges.

trip to nebraska

Make it recycled using an old atlas or map. To soften the effect, place a vellum square on point over the background, allowing the corners of the map to show brilliantly.

QUICK TIP

Turn vellum on point (to make a diamond) to soften part of the background.

Complement the travel theme with a map section from the highlighted area.

Print the headline on white paper, leaving room for a photo.

Glue colorful die-cuts at the top and bottom of the page.

Secure vellum in the center, fold the corners to the back, and tape.

materials

- photo
- 12-inch square of orange card stock
- 10½×12-inch rectangle from atlas or map
- 12-inch square of vellum
- 8×9-inch piece of textured turquoise paper
- white printer paper
- 2 daisy die-cuts
- paper trimmer
- computer and printer
- tape
- adhesive

great-grandmother

Use vellum stickers to secure a journal box.

Make it heartwarming by applying vellum stickers to accent the headline and the journal box. Vellum offers subtle color and design while allowing the background to show through.

materials

- photos
- 12-inch square of green card stock
- yellow card stock
- vellum
- vellum stickers
- chalk in black and dark yellow
- computer and printer
- paper trimmer
- adhesive

Overlap one or two stickers on each journal box.

Print type on vellum and chalk the edges for character.

Place the photos at the top and balance with the headline at the bottom.

grampa's lake

Make it unified by butting photos together to create a square. Separate the photos by adhering decorative strips over the seams. All the art embellishments for this page, including the plaid strips, are provided on *page 311.*

Use the stick art from page 311 to form a border around photos.

Center the journal box at the bottom of the page.

Write your headline and journaling with marking pens.

QUICK TIP

Use scissors to cut out the plaid strips within the heavy black outlines.

materials

- photos
- 12-inch square of green watercolor-style scrapbook paper
- color photocopy of desired art on page 311
- scissors
- paper trimmer
- wide-tip green marking pen
- fine-line black marking pen
- adhesive

Art in back of book!

see page 311

a day at the hangar

Make it picture-packed by trimming each photo to eliminate uninteresting space where possible and/or overlapping photos to cover uninteresting areas. Use narrow mats to keep photos as large

materials

- photos
- two 12-inch squares of cloud background paper
- red and white paper
- paper cutter
- crafts knife
- decorative-edge scissors
- red marking pen
- lettering stencil
- adhesive

Write journaling in red on white paper and cut with scalloped scissors.

The position of faces, arrangement of shapes, and curvy line help the flow of this layout.

as possible. Angle photos slightly for a "free-falling" look. Create the headline using a stencil and pen. Write all the journaling in puffy paper clouds that trail from the silhouette of the plane.

QUICK TIP

Silhouette items to add to the composition.

Create a headline with a stencil and marking pen.

Cloud paper is the perfect choice for pages with an airplane theme.

QUICK TIP

Place stickers on cream card stock and chalk the edges for a vintage look.

moving day

Make it timely using photocopies of newspaper clippings. Combine them with present photos for an interesting collage.

materials

- photos
- photocopy of newspaper clipping
- 12-inch square of white card stock
- card stock in brown, black, dark olive, and cream
- alphabet, numeral, and embellishment stickers
- date stamp
- paper trimmer
- brown chalk
- adhesive

Place alphabet stickers in a wavy fashion.

Angle a newspaper clipping for drama.

Align photos vertically on the right-hand side.

national guard

Make it honorable by combining a die-cut headline, an enlarged photo, tags, dimensional stickers, mesh, and theme-print paper to capture the effect. Minimal trimming and premade embellishments help the page move along quickly.

QUICK TIP

Personalize a plain tag using alphabet and word stickers.

Create texture with a wide strip of mesh.

Overlay the headline in the center of the page

Handwrite journaling on the photo.

Trim top paper and align with the bottom right corner of the coordinating paper.

materials

- photo
- two 12-inch squares of coordinating scrapbook papers
- 6½×12-inch piece of black adhesive mesh
- die-cut headline
- 2 metal tags on ball chain
- black alphabet and word stickers with clear background
- dimensional military-theme stickers
- date stamp
- black fine-line marking pen
- scissors
- adhesive

honorable duty

Make it patriotic with a waving flag in the background. To re-create the look, enlarge the patterns on *page 271* at 670 percent. Cut out the pieces and trace onto red and blue papers. Cut out the blue corner an red stripes. Using the pattern as a guide, glue the pieces on parchmen

Punch stars between the letters for detail.

Choose a bold computer type and print on vellum to allow the flag motif to show through.

materials

- photos
- tracing paper
- pencil; scissors
- 12-inch square of parchment paper
- 12-inch squares of red and blue textured-looking papers
- 8½×11-inch pieces of vellum
- computer and printer
- star paper punch
- ⅛-inch-wide double-stick tape
- round black shank buttons with star inserts
- thick white crafts glue
- wire cutters
- vintage-style decorative-edge scissors
- photocopies of war-related items, such as letters, medals, papers, books, diaries, etcetera
- adhesive

QUICK TIP

Use wire cutters to remove the shanks from star buttons.

Use vellum to back the headline, allowing the background to subtly show through. Arrange the photos and memorabilia on the page. To accent the headline use layered round and star buttons or paper circles with star stickers.

Select muted colors to symbolize the American flag without overpowering the photos.

Carefully place memorabilia to reveal important dates or words.

Pattern in back of book!

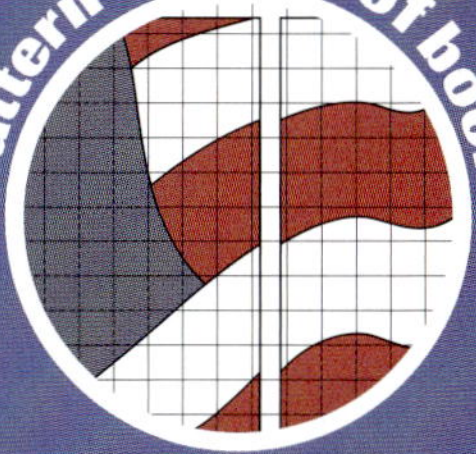

see page 271

our new harley

Make it bold using black and white photos. To get a striking look, mount photos on black paper and trim. Create contrast using different colors of paper for the left and right pages. Print the main headline in white on a black background. Print the subheads in black

materials

- photos
- 12-inch squares of background paper in coordinating colors
- bike tire
- black stamp pad
- orange acrylic paint and paintbrush
- black paper
- crafts knife or scissors
- paper cutter
- computer and printer
- white or colored paper
- permanent marking pens
- adhesive

Use a bold, colorful headline to draw attention and lead into the main photo.

Use a computer to generate easy-to-read journaling.

on white. Color in the white areas using yellow and orange marking pens. To make tire tracks, roll a bike tire on an ink pad, then roll the tire on the paper. Overlap another track or two and don't worry about smudges—they add to the look.

QUICK TIP

To make tire tracks, roll a clean and dry tire across an ink pad or paint and then roll across the paper.

Line up top of headline with top of photo for an orderly appearance. Trim photos to the same size, keeping unity in an asymmetrical layout.

QUICK TIP

Place a border around the page to help maintain order.

mom the artist

Make it flashy using colorful elements tied together with good design. Use a variety of sizes and silhouetted shapes for interest. Choose one large item to focus on, as was done with the man in the moon. Include one or two rectangular shapes so the design is not overly busy.

materials

- photos
- variety of colored papers
- appropriate paper for border
- watercolor paper
- crafts knife
- scissors
- paper cutter
- alphabet template
- pencil
- fine-point markers
- colored pencils
- adhesive

Use an appropriate border paper that relates to the theme.

Mount a rectangular photo on an irregular mat.

Lightly color in some of open space with colored pencil.

Layer letters on random colorful paper shapes for a dramatic headline.

little cookies

Make it tasteful using a cookie recipe and photos of the family making the delicious treats. Use several photos, a headline, journaling, and the recipe in a grid fashion for a full but balanced page.

QUICK TIP

Sew silver charms to small card stock rectangles and to the recipe.

Stitch the edges together for a two-tone mounting piece.

Glue buttons with knotted thread to the headline corners.

Apply pink and yellow chalk to white card stock for a subtle appearance.

Omit matting for closeup photos.

materials

- recipe
- photos
- 12-inch square of pink, green, and white stripe paper
- card stock in pink, green, and white
- chalk in yellow and pink
- ¼-inch green buttons
- thread in pink and green
- needle
- silver charms with cooking theme
- computer and printer
- paper cutter
- thick white crafts glue
- adhesive

family reunions

Make it photo-packed by adhering mini flip books on each page. This is the perfect answer when you have lots of pictures to include but lack enough pages in your scrapbook. To make each mini flip

Layer three-ring binder pages to create mini books.

Use eyelets as decorative accents on journaling boxes.

materials

- photos
- 12-inch squares of background paper
- vellum
- watercolor pencils
- blender pen
- eyelets
- eyelet tool
- paper punch
- ivy cutouts
- rose stencil
- scissors
- photo album pages in desired sizes
- sewing machine and thread
- adhesive

book, remove pages from a photo album. Stack several sheets and sew them onto card stock using a sewing machine, then adhere the stack to a page.

Use watercolor pencils to color in headlines and stencils.

QUICK TIP

Computer-generate a headline and color it in using watercolor pencils that coordinate with the photos and page theme. Use a blender pen to blend the pencil colors.

happily ever after

Make it formal with two coordinating elegant background papers. The common deep red hue of these papers creates compatibility between the pages, but you can choose whatever colors were used in your wedding. Use a busier pattern and wide mat behind a single

materials

- photos
- two 12-inch squares of coordinating patterned papers
- vellum
- paper cutter or crafts knife and ruler
- ivory lace adhesive border
- embossed ivory paper
- solid-color papers in burgundy and ivory
- decorative corner paper punch
- alphabet stickers
- adhesive

Use translucent paper, lace, and embossed ivory paper to make beautiful wedding pages.

Choose papers similar to the decor of the wedding to complement the photos.

photo. For smaller photos, choose a more monotone background. To back the lettering, use a triangle and a square tipped on point. Center metallic sticker letters within the shapes to add sparkle to a wedding day collection of photos.

QUICK TIP

For added elegance cut translucent paper into a square and place on point to soften the pattern behind the photo.

Use a decorative corner punch to allow background paper to show through.

Create a formal, symmetrical design with squares.

Crop similar small photos and arrange as windowpanes.

liljander

Make it family-oriented with the family name boldly stated in a headline. To create it print out the name. Transfer the letters to white paper and cut out using a crafts knife. Tape brown paper beneath the cutout letters. Use the pattern on *page 270* to make the tree from

Use a computer to generate a pattern for the headline.

Crop, layer, and glue to make quick photo mats.

Repeat patterned papers throughout the layout.

materials

- photos
- tracing paper
- pencil
- crafts knife
- straightedge
- transfer paper
- tape
- two 12-inch squares of white card stock
- two 11½-inch squares of light blue textured paper
- 8½×11-inch piece of patterned brown paper
- 12-inch squares of three or more patterned green papers
- paper cutter
- computer and printer
- photocopies of items
- black fine-line marking pen
- adhesive

QUICK TIP

Use paper scraps to make photo corners.

white paper. Back the openings with patterned green and brown papers taped in place. Carefully silhouette photocopies of family memorabilia and label with handwritten journaling.

Photocopy meaningful items and crop silhouette style.

Record tidbits of information in handwritten notes.

Use the pattern on page 270 to make a quiltlike family tree.

Pattern in back of book!

see page 270

the little flower

QUICK TIP

Apply a sheet of vellum over a photo to soften its appearance.

Make it documented by including a story from a family member as journaling. Combine the story with a photo of the author and something to visually tie in with the story, enlarging the image if necessary to fill the background.

materials

- photos
- 12-inch square of background card stock
- 12-inch square of vellum
- embossed paper with frames
- computer, printer, and colored paper
- white opaque marking pen
- crafts knife
- adhesive

Cut a romantic oval mat to flatter a vintage photo.

Use adhesive between photo and vellum only where it will be covered by the narrow mat.

Write the title using an opaque marking pen.

Frame the story using solid-color papers.

sisters

Make it feminine using luscious colors, soft textures, dainty details, and hints of sparkle to frame a black and white photo of women. This page involves floral stickers with gem embellishments, a sheer ribbon bow, and a mix of papers including floral, metallic, and velvet.

Use die-cut stickers to add floral accents.

Use sheer ribbon so it will lie flat when the book is closed.

Use adhesive stickers for a simple headline.

Use decorative-edge scissors for a vintage look.

QUICK TIP

Make framing a breeze with a purchased mat.

materials

- photo
- 12-inch square of patterned plum paper
- 12-inch square of lavender velvet embossed paper
- 8½×11-inch green, plum, and lavender floral paper
- 8½×11-inch lavender and metallic gold print paper
- periwinkle floral stickers
- plum precut mat
- 1-inch-wide sheer green ribbon
- scissors
- paper cutter
- decorative-edge scissors
- alphabet stickers
- adhesive

brothers

Make it symmetrical on the left page and asymmetrical on the right. This formula works well for four photos as shown. To spice up the layout, create layered photo mats using a combination of striped

materials

- photos
- 12-inch squares of burgundy paper
- red polka-dot paper
- red striped paper
- tan linen paper
- sheer ribbon
- paper tags
- chalk
- rub-on ivy, morning glory, and hummingbird motifs
- paper cutter
- computer and printer
- adhesive

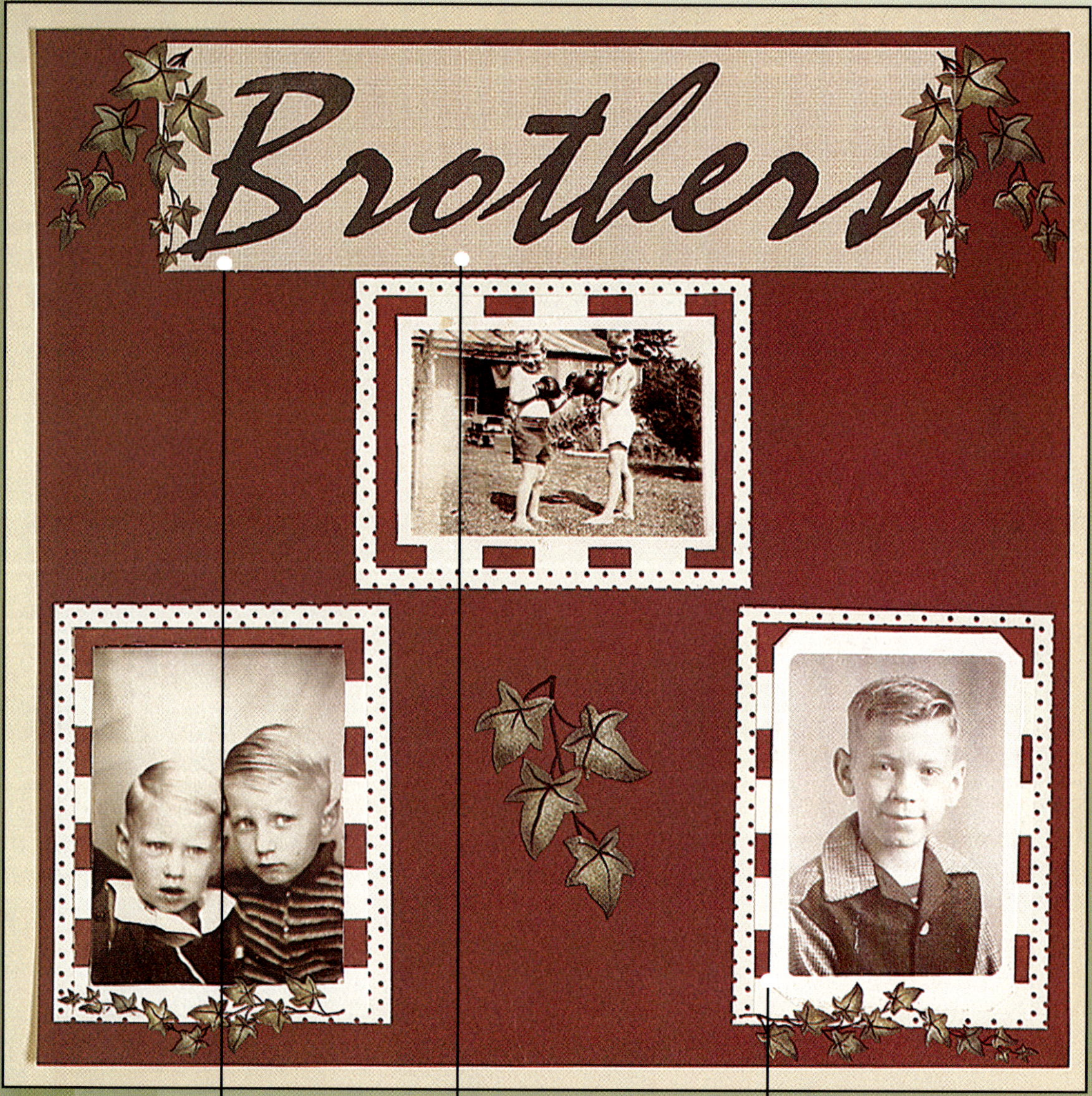

Print the headline in dark green to coordinate with the ivy.

Cut 12-inch-square paper to 8½×11 inches to fit through a printer.

Turn striped paper vertically and horizontally for interesting mats.

QUICK TIP

Chalk the tag edges for a vintage look.

and polka-dot papers. To vary the stripe turn it to make vertical stripes for the mat on the top photo. Accent the pages with stickers, enveloping the headline as well as photos.

Use rub-on motifs as decorative elements on each page.

fishing kids

Make it lively using animated drawing, angled photos, and whimsical journaling. To create the bobber, hook, and worm, trace the patterns on *page 275* onto white paper. Color the pieces as desired. Cut out shapes. Add blue chalk to shade in the area near the silhouette of

materials

- photos
- light mottled green paper
- contrasting paper to mount photos
- paper cutter or crafts knife
- soft blue chalk
- red and white paper
- opaque marking pens in black, red, and white
- scissors
- adhesive

Create easy freehand journaling with a black marking pen. Go over with a white opaque marking pen, leaving a black shadow on bottom and left.

Tilt photos at various angles to add to the playfulness of the page.

the large fish. Draw white bubbles by the fish and affix the worm, hook, and bobber. Pen the fishing line, arrange and label the photos, and this page is both fun and done.

QUICK TIP

Crop around a person to break out of a photo box.

Scrape blue chalk with a crafts knife and blend in the dust with a cotton ball to create a water effect.

Include all the participants when telling a fishing tale.

Silhouette an image that depicts the pages' theme.

Patterns in back of book!

see page 275

Calling all animal lovers! These clever pages will get you scrapbooking quicker than you can say, “Sit! Stay! Roll over!”

creatures great and small

QUICK TIP

Ask your photo developer to print photos with a white edge to save time matting.

croppy cat

Make it stickered by arranging alphabet stickers in a wavy fashion to make headline placement easy. For added charm use theme stickers across the top of the page and at corners of the journal box.

materials

- 12-inch squares of card stock in green and white
- card stock scraps in dark red, green, and gold
- checked scrapbook paper
- small silver brads
- alphabet stickers
- scrapbook-theme stickers
- small paper punch
- computer and printer
- paper trimmer
- adhesive

Anchor a checked strip with stickers.

Use a larger and bolder font for the journaling subhead.

Cut journal box large enough to overlap a corner with stickers.

all I need to know

Make it a quick read using several short journal boxes. Print dark type on white paper, crop boxes into small rectangles, and overlap dead photo areas for playful positioning.

QUICK TIP

Offset a 10-inch square of contrasting paper to jazz up the background.

Mount a sticker on layered card stock.

Overlap photos with labels.

Make your headline look like a sign by placing two small rectangles and brads at the top of the headline block.

materials

- photos
- 12-inch square of navy card stock
- 10-inch square of dark red card stock
- scraps of card stock in white, blue, and dark red
- square brads
- paw print sticker
- computer and printer
- small paper punch
- paper trimmer
- adhesive

penny and frieda

Make it heartfelt by writing journaling as a story or poem and accent the page with heart motifs. To make the heart mats, use the pattern on *page 274*, enlarging the pattern 200 percent. To make the large heart mat, cut a 6½-inch square from black swirl paper using

materials

- photos
- 12-inch squares of ocher background paper
- black and white swirled-pattern paper
- red star paper
- pink parchment paper
- black paper
- computer and printer
- tracing paper
- pencil
- pink, black, and white opaque marking pens
- pinking shears
- crafts knife
- paper cutter
- adhesive

Cut out several small paper hearts drawn freehand.

Enlarge and crop one main photo for the left page.

pinking shears. Turn the square on point and trace the larger heart. Cut out with a crafts knife. Cut the inner mat using the small heart pattern. Trim to fit behind the black mat. Cut the smaller hearts from pink and black papers.

Write a poem for extra-interesting journaling.

Trim all photo mats to the same size for consistency.

QUICK TIP

Use opaque markers to create a stylish, colorful headline.

Pattern in back of book!

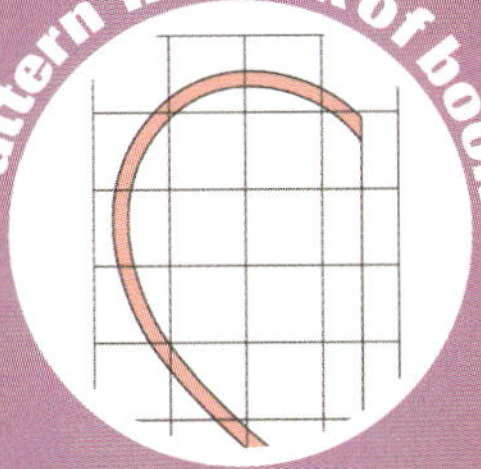

see page 274

QUICK TIP

Place contrasting strips on the top and bottom of the page to keep photos from floating.

materials

- **photos**
- **paper cutter**
- **scissors or crafts knife**
- **black marker**
- **8½×11-inch piece of background paper with a subtle pattern, such as gray checks**
- **patterned black paper**
- **black paper**
- **coordinating pattern paper for title**
- **alphabet stickers**
- **adhesive**

anne and rascal

Make it pop using two similar photos in different ways to tell a story. To draw attention to a particular photo, enlarge it dramatically and cut away the unnecessary background.

Allow white space to subtly break up the background pattern.

Enlarge and silhouette a photo for drama.

Use colorful initials to carry out the artistic look and to coordinate with hand-lettering.

tink

Make it focused with a single photo and a layering of mats in shades of one color. Keep journaling to a minimum and accent the page with dimensional stickers.

Add decorative photo corners as finishing touches.

Choose subtle accent papers to avoid overpowering the photo.

Repeat the oval shape for the journal box below.

Use floral paper embellishments for easy elegance.

QUICK TIP

Create the oval mat using a swivel oval template and blade.

materials

- photo
- four varying shades of green paper
- ivory textured paper
- paper cutter
- oval template
- swivel blade
- ruler
- computer and printer
- paper floral photo corners and die cuts
- adhesive

Outline your own art elements with a wide black marking pen to make cropping easy.

my cat

Make it vivid with a large colorful photo frame and a single photo. The pretty frame, headline, and journal heart are provided on *pages 313* and *315.* Photocopy the art elements to use them several times.

materials

- photo
- 12-inch square of blue polka-dot paper
- color photocopy of art, pages 313 and 315
- scissors
- black marking pen
- tape
- adhesive

Use scissors to cut a slightly wavy line around art elements from pages 313 and 315.

Use a marking pen for personalization.

Glue the photo and frame slightly below the page center.

see pages 313 and 315

cat sitter

Make it purr by combining cat embellishments with solid color papers. The print elements, *below*, are available on *page 319*. Team these charming accents with blues and tans for a beautifully quick page.

QUICK TIP

Use a paper punch to make a starter hole for eyelets.

Use a star punch to make accents from yellow paper.

Place the darkest color of card stock on the bottom of the page for weight.

Leave a photo unmounted if it contrasts with the paper color.

materials

- photos
- 12-inch squares of 3 coordinating scrapbook papers, plus white and yellow
- color photocopy of art elements, page 319
- round and star paper punches
- eyelets and eyelet tool
- scissors
- light blue fibers
- computer and printer
- black fine-line marking pen
- paper trimmer
- adhesive

Art in back of book!

see page 319

QUICK TIP

Cut several card stock strips at one sitting to have readily available.

tinsel

Make it catchy using a subhead to direct the page. Look at advertisements and watch commercials for inspiration; then continue the thought in the journaling.

materials

- photos
- 12-inch square of white card stock
- 12×6¼-inch rectangle of teal card stock
- card stock in black and white
- teal brads
- small paper punch
- paper trimmer
- computer and printer
- adhesive

Crop three photos the same height and align side by side.

Cut two strips and join end to end to run the width of the page.

Leave room below the title for a block of journaling.

our dog t-bone

Make it bordered by using premade heart and triangle strips. The versatile borders at the top and bottom of this page are available on *page 276.*

Print the headline and journaling on vellum; crop to desired size.

Incorporate a sticker into the headline.

Use marking pens to color in a copy of the border from page 276.

QUICK TIP

Layer precut color card stock squares and place behind a photo to draw attention to it.

materials

- photo
- 12-inch square of yellow card stock
- 12×5-inch rectangle of grass-print paper
- 2½-inch square of red card stock
- 3-inch square of orange card stock
- 4½-inch square of yellow card stock
- 3×4-inch piece of red card stock
- vellum; color marking pens
- photocopies of border pattern, page 276
- dog-theme die cuts and dimensional stickers; scissors
- computer and printer
- spray adhesive
- adhesive

Pattern in back of book!

see page 276

QUICK TIP

Separate the words of the headline to frame the top and bottom of the page.

materials

- photos
- 12-inch squares of patterned paper
- flannel paper
- lettering template
- water-drop stickers
- oval template
- punches
- fiber
- vellum
- adhesive

bath-time blues

Make it comical with a catchy headline. Cut the letters using a template and add wavy fibers behind the words at the top and bottom of the page.

Use an oval template ensure edges that are smooth.

Apply water-drop stickers around journaling and on top of photos.

Use vellum to overlay the background and make journaling easier to read.

A patterned paper works well for a bathing theme.

day in the field

Make it outdoorsy using premade sketched nature mats and borders. These wildlife designs are on *page 321* to photocopy and use again and again.

Use a crafts knife to cut out the center of the mat.

Cut a photo into a diamond shape and mount on a colored piece of paper.

Computer-generate the headline and trace the outline onto the background papers.

QUICK TIP

Cut a triangle from contrasting paper, overlap, and write the headline across both papers.

materials

- photos
- 12-inch square of paper to coordinate with art, page 329
- $8\frac{1}{2}\times11$-inch piece of paper to contrast background paper
- green scrapbook paper
- color photocopy of desired art, page 321
- crafts knife
- computer and printer
- tracing paper; pencil
- green colored pencil
- adhesive

Art in back of book!

see page 321

best friend

Make it look professional using just the right photo mats, journal boxes, and headlines to help your pet photos shine. The art provided on *page 323* will help you create your own pet page. Trim away the inside of the doghouse and use as a photo mat. Use

Silhouette a single puppy in proportion to the doghouse size.

Use the doghouse art as a photo mat.

Personalize the doughouse by printing the name of your dog.

materials

- photos
- two 11×8½-inch pieces of green background paper
- photocopies of art on page 323
- scissors
- crafts knife
- metal ruler
- black fine-line marking pen
- adhesive

the coordinating headline, mats, and journal boxes to complete scrapbook pages in a hurry. For more extensive journaling write copy in blocks in the open areas of the background using a contrasting color of ink.

Use a black marking pen to create striking journaling against the watercolor label.

Use a ruler and crafts knife to cut straight edges.

QUICK TIP

Photocopy the desired art elements full size or reduce or enlarge them to fit your photographs.

Art in back of book!

see page 323

QUICK TIP

Offset journal strips on darker card stock rectangles to create the look of a shadow.

materials

- large photo
- 12-inch square of gold subtle-print scrapbook paper
- purple scrapbook paper
- white paper
- mulberry papers in black and metallic brown
- purple marking pen
- computer and printer
- paper trimmer
- adhesive

polly and emma

Make it humorous using one large photo and labels printed from a computer. A lighthearted photo works well with this layout and is enhanced by the jesting option statements at the top of the page.

Type a check-off box before each statement.

Tear and layer mulberry paper to resemble dirt.

Mount the photo and journaling on contrasting papers.

emma and honey

Make it in minutes with copy, cut, and use photo frames. These coordinating frames are provided on *pages 313* and *317*. Cut them out and layer them on additional papers to make the page rich with color.

Punch a hole in the top edge of the tag. Thread ribbon through a jumpring; attach the tag.

Fold ribbon back and forth vertically on the page, adhering in spots with glue stick.

Trim a wider green mat to back the provided decorative mat. Cut out the frame center using a crafts knife.

QUICK TIP

Use a loop of gold jumpring to hang a paper tag from ½-inch-wide ribbon.

materials

- photos
- 12-inch square of green polka-dot paper
- rust subtle-pattern scrapbook paper
- dark green card stock
- color photocopy of mats and tag, pages 313 and 317
- ½-inch-wide gold and burgundy ribbon
- gold jumpring
- paper punch
- paper trimmer
- black marking pen
- crafts knife
- adhesive

Art in back of book!

see pages 313 and 317

me and my horses

Make it photo rich and full of happy childhood memories using multiple photos. Whether you or your little one has horses or kitties, be sure to take and use plenty of snapshots to recall those joyous times together. Choose a patterned paper that relates to the animal

materials

- photos
- 12-inch squares of wheat-print background paper
- paper cutter
- papers in green, gold, and brown
- decorative-edge scissors
- green sticker lettering
- green opaque marking pen
- adhesive

Use a photo, such as this horse's head, that leads into the layout.

Apply stickers side by side and overlap them for interest.

and use it for the background. To make the photos stand out, mat them separately or in groupings on paper that contrasts with the background. Make simple labels or use one of the photo spots for more journaling.

QUICK TIP

Group photos on one panel for extraquick matting.

Line up edges neatly for an orderly page.

Use decorative scissors to create interesting shapes for journal boxes.

QUICK TIP

"Ground" animal stickers and die cuts by placing them on torn paper "grass."

ride 'em, cowboy

Make it matted by aligning the photos on one card stock rectangle. This presentation groups the photos as a unit to create a clean layout.

materials

- photos
- 12-inch square of leatherlike navy blue card stock
- card stock in tan and two shades of green
- 12-inch strip of ½-inch-wide stitched suede trim
- horse die cut
- computer and printer
- corner rounder
- paper trimmer
- thick white crafts glue
- adhesive

Use crafts glue to hold suede trim in place.

Combine headline fonts for interest.

Use a corner rounder on the headline paper.

Tear a piece of green paper to look like grass.

animal rescue

Make it color-blocked using a simple technique in which blocks of solid-color or print papers are placed in a random pattern to create a background or photo mat. Adhere the blocks of color on your page to create an interesting background that coordinates with photos.

QUICK TIP

Allow the color blocks to back most of the photos.

Print the headline and journaling on a light color.

Select three to four colors from the photos and choose paper and card stock to match.

Place coordinating stickers diagonally on the page to add movement.

Balance the colors and shapes in the layout.

materials

- photos
- 12-inch square of gold card stock
- card stock in green, white, and black
- paw print stickers
- computer and printer
- paper trimmer
- adhesive

2003 Iowa State Fair Chili Cook-Off

August, 2003

As told by Jay Petersma, Judge

good tasting

lo

Hip...hip...hooray!
Share life's happiest
moments with
imaginative ideas
that are just as fun
as the events
themselves.

time to celebrate

QUICK TIP

Eliminate matting by leaving a white edge when cutting around stamps.

blossoming music

Make it decorative with rubber-stamped embellishments. You can create an endless array of designs by changing the ink colors to complement your theme.

materials

- photos
- 12-inch square of white card stock
- 12-inch square of royal blue card stock
- 12-inch square of blue print paper
- scraps of card stock in black and white
- flower rubber stamp
- ink pads in blue, black, and yellow
- black brads
- ¾-inch black alphabet stickers
- ribbon memento
- scissors
- small paper punch
- paper trimmer
- computer and printer
- adhesive
- adhesive spacers, such as Pop Dots

Use brads or black card stock triangles in each corner.

Mat photos simply using black and white card stock.

Apply alphabet stickers on scrapbook paper and tear the edges.

celebration

Make it animated by placing photos of guests' heads on drawn stick figures. To get the look, enlarge the pattern on *page 273* on a photocopier. Trace the design on tracing paper. Place transfer paper between pattern and black paper; retrace with a dressmaker's pencil.

Place alphabet stickers in a wavy line to enliven headline.

Use cardboard key rings to make ready-made frames for head shots.

Use a dressmaker's pencil on black paper.

Draw lines for balloon strings.

QUICK TIP

Use a round template slightly smaller than the tag, such as a coin, as a pattern to draw circles around the faces.

materials

- photos
- tracing paper
- pencil
- white transfer paper
- 12-inch square of black paper
- white dressmaker's pencil
- cardboard key-ring tag with wire removed (available at office supply stores)
- round template
- alphabet stickers
- balloon stickers
- scissors
- adhesive

Pattern in back of book!

see page 273

QUICK TIP

Buy two-tone card stock (a different color on each side) to simplify paper selection and multiply options.

materials

- photos
- 12-inch square of white card stock
- card stock in purple, pink, and white
- 12-inch square of pink heart-print paper
- alphabet die-cut machine
- computer and printer
- paper punch
- adhesive

sweet hearts

Make it patterned and solid by mixing strips of scrapbook paper and card stock as the starting point for an effective design. Buy premade strips or cut your own. This technique is a handy way to use leftover paper and rations your paper over multiple pages.

Tear a wide strip of print paper for the left side and back it with two narrow strips of card stock.

Use a very wide block of one color on the bottom half of the layout.

Use a die-cut machine to customize a coordinating headline.

Cut an element from print paper to make an embellishment.

on her way

Make it matted using premade frames to immediately give a professional look to your page. Scrapbooking stores carry a variety of frames, including solids, prints, and themes. Frame sets make for even easier scrapbooking.

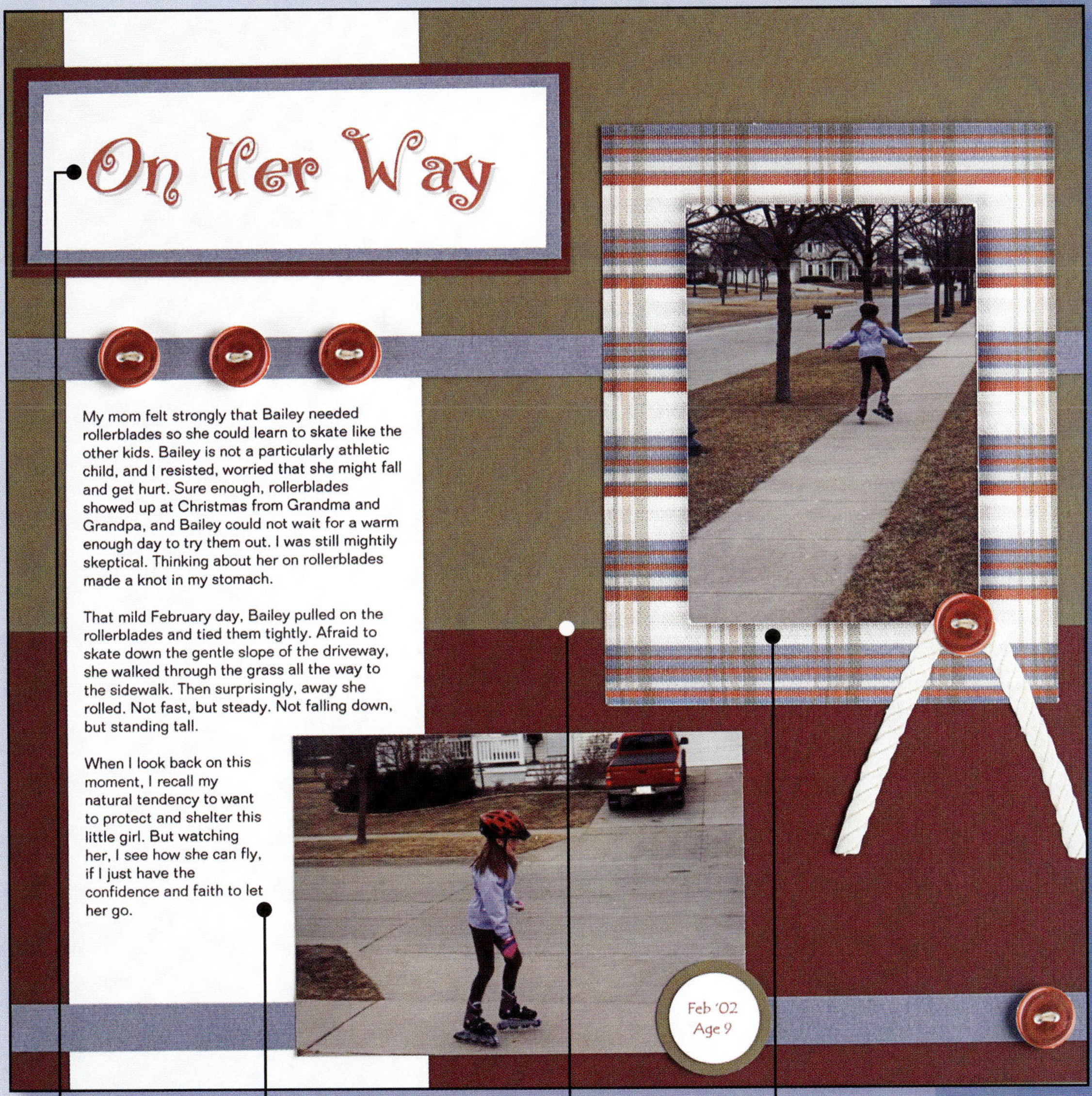

Print the headline in matching ink or use alphabet stickers.

Print journaling, leaving a wide space for a headline.

Split the background into two colors to add interest.

Coordinate the background paper with the frame and photos.

QUICK TIP

If the frame cutout is too small, mount the photo angled on top of the frame.

materials

- photos
- 12-inch square of olive card stock
- 12-inch square of wine card stock
- card stock in blue and white
- plaid premade photo frame
- button stickers
- circle punch in two sizes
- computer and printer
- paper trimmer
- adhesive

tea for two hundred

Make it gilded using metallic gold for journal framing, stamping, writing, and stickers to help hold the invitation clippings in place. Team up the metallic color with navy or other dark tones for a striking formal appearance. Make two pages appear to be connected

Incorporate tiny art elements to add style to plain boxes.

Photocopy parts of an invitation to set the stage for the theme.

Handwrite the headline in gold ink on blue paper and trim close to the lettering.

materials

- photos
- two 12-inch squares of neutral patterned papers
- two $8\frac{1}{2}\times11$-inch pieces of red and gold formal papers
- papers in navy blue, white, metallic gold, and red
- rubber stamps in teapot, teacup, and spoon designs
- metallic gold ink pad
- metallic gold marking pen
- emblem stickers
- paper cutter or crafts knife and ruler
- scissors
- blue fine-line marking pen
- party invitation
- adhesive

by placing a contrasting paper across the center of two pages and by using triangles to cover each outer corner of the pages. Use mats to set off the invitation and journaling and group photos for organized appeal.

QUICK TIP

Trim stamped images just beyond the stamped edge to appear as a die cut on the page.

Stamp navy paper with gold ink to create a formal look.

Stamp extra paper to add decorative details.

classic cars

Make it exciting using several photos of details organized onto panels matted on black. Silhouetted items, such as the top row of cars, work better on a busy layout when they appear in one area.

materials

- photos
- 12-inch squares of silver-gray background paper
- black paper
- red metallic adhesive-backed paper
- computer and printer
- scissors
- crafts knife
- black dimensional paint pen
- adhesive

Group detail shots to make an organized layout.

Back detail shots with a solid-color paper for unity.

Type the headline on a computer and use a mirror setting to print it. Cut and peel off a section of vinyl large enough to apply to the back of the printed headline. Trim the words closely with scissors. Use adhesive on the paper side to affix the words to the layout.

Silhouette a large main photo to draw attention to it on a photo-packed page.

Create a bold, glitzy headline using a computer font and metallic paper to give the pages a focal point. Handwrite the label by a photo with people in it to complete the page with personality plus.

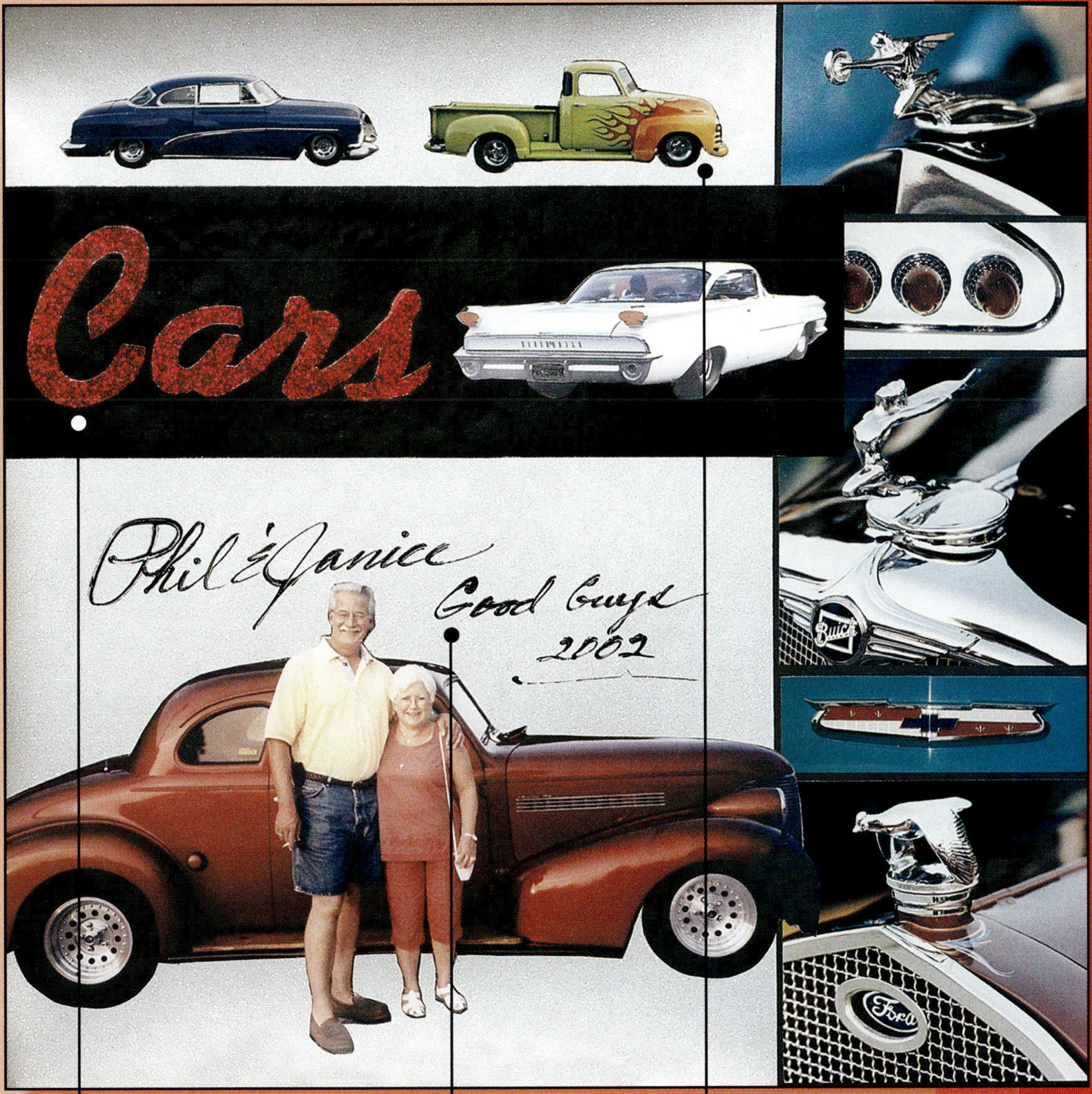

Use metallic vinyl for a showy headline.

Keep journaling simple on a busy layout.

Place silhouettes in a row to avoid clutter.

Use an oval cutter to create a simple egg and then use scissors to cut a zigzag across the center.

easter eggs

Make it eggs-tra sweet using silhouetted children's photos that seem to interact with one another. Enlarge the photos first, if necessary, to fit the desired size oval egg.

materials

- photos
- 12-inch square of yellow polka-dot paper
- 12-inch square of green patterned paper
- sticker letters
- white card stock
- oval cutter
- colored pencils in pink, yellow, and green
- photocopier or scanner and printer
- scissors
- adhesive

Draw simple designs on eggshells that are inspired by the pattern in the headline.

Choose background paper with a subtle design.

Choose papers to coordinate with the die-cut letters.

Position photos to interact with each other to create personality.

happy easter

Make it quick as a bunny using a scrapbooking page kit that provides coordinating headlines, corners, die cuts, embellishments, mats, and journal boxes. If you wish customize your page by incorporating your own supplies.

QUICK TIP

Use the corners from the kit to frame the page.

Split the color of the background.

Print journaling on vellum and mat on the box provided or write directly on the journal box.

Contribute elements that correspond to the premade items, such as the torn strip of yellow layered on orange at the page bottom.

Print journaling and punch out a circle to make a tag; embellish with fiber.

materials

- photos
- 12-inch squares of card stock in yellow, lime green, orange, orange-yellow, and white
- Easter scrapbooking page kit
- paper trimmer
- adhesive

QUICK TIP

Before choosing background paper, color in the designs and mount your photos. Bring those elements with you to select paper.

materials

- photos
- photocopy of patterns, page 325
- 12-inch square of background paper
- colored marking pens
- crafts knife
- paper cutter
- adhesive

Art to color in back of book!

see page 325

graduation day

Make it customized with class colors and unique journaling. The mats and headlines found here are provided in black and white on *page 325.* Scan or photocopy these art pieces and color them in with marking pens, reducing or enlarging the elements to fit your page.

Create your own year with the numbers from page 325.

Use school colors to personalize the black and white mat design. Enlarge the best photo to draw the most attention.

Personalize a mini diploma to capture the importance of the day.

Fourth of july

Make it primarily primary with white background paper and a trio of primary colors that seem to dance on the page. Generate a coordinating headline on a computer and cut it out using large zigzag cuts.

QUICK TIP

Use colorful stars to act as confetti on the page. Punch them from the papers used behind the headline.

materials

- photos
- 12-inch square of white card stock
- card stock mats in primary-colors
- star patterned papers
- computer and printer
- chalk
- star punch
- adhesive

Angle 2-inch paper squares to frame the headline.

Print the headline on a computer and trim using random zigzag cuts.

Use precut mats to make photo mounting easy.

Silhouette photos to add dramatic interest to the page.

happy birthday

Make it pop up with a dimensional piece that looks like a slice of cake. To make it, copy the patterns on *page 272* at 200 percent on a photocopier. Trace around the cake pattern on confetti paper and the candles on contrasting paper; cut out shapes. Create lettering on a computer, print it, and color it in using a marking pen.

materials

- photos
- tracing paper
- pencil
- two 12-inch squares of white background paper
- balloon pattern paper
- confetti paper
- blue floral paper
- goldenrod paper
- chalk
- party hat die cut
- numeral punch
- marking pen
- journal balloons
- scissors
- double-sided tape
- adhesive

Silhouette photos to provide focus on the subject matter.

Use two thicknesses of paper to support the pop-up center.

Blend colored chalk around the edges of the balloon shapes to soften the look.

Secure the pop-up with tacky double-sided tape.

Cut solid yellow inner mats to separate the photos from the busy outer mats and background paper.

see page 272

birthday bash

Make it striped using broad paper strips to create a fun, yet organized background. Choose the background papers, die cut, and frames at the same time to coordinate the colors. Use balloon buttons in the same colors as the paper accents to help

materials

- photos
- 12-inch squares of card stock in blue, green, and goldenrod
- frames and die cuts
- balloon buttons
- fibers
- foam squares
- scissors
- adhesive

Trim the headline lettering, leaving a narrow white border to separate it from the background.

Angle photos in different directions to balance the left and right pages.

Add dimension by using balloon buttons mounted on foam squares.

frame the main photos, allowing them to float as if filled with helium. Tie the fibers to appear as the balloon strings and thread through the holes of the balloons.

QUICK TIP

Purchase colorblocked paper to saving cutting time and paper costs.

Cut apart die cuts to make three candles for the cupcake.

Use a computer font for journaling.

Tie long threads to the balloons in groups of two or three.

state fair

Make it a mirror-image background to connect pages in a spread. Highlight an element from the photos for artistic embellishments. The tents in these photos are easily re-created from

materials

- photos
- two 12-inch squares of dark blue card stock
- 12-inch squares of card stock in green, red, white, and yellow
- chile pepper sticker
- square punch
- computer and printer
- paper trimmer
- scissors
- adhesive

Print headline and journaling on one piece of paper and crop around blocks.

Embellish pages with punched squares, turning some on point.

simple paper shapes. Arrange the photos differently on each page to keep the layout interesting. Punched squares add polish to the design by sprinkling it with accents of red.

QUICK TIP

August, 2003

Use logos provided on a related website to accent a page.

Place paper rectangles on the inside edges to unify pages.

Leave most photos uncropped, matting only two.

QUICK TIP

Use a photo marker to color in an important part of the photo, such as these pumpkins.

the great pumpkin

Make it folded by cutting the mat larger on one side and folding that edge over the photo. To embellish, trim the flap with brads, stickers, or other desired elements.

materials

- black and white photos
- 12-inch square of orange plaid paper
- thin cardboard
- orange small-print paper
- newsprint scrapbook paper
- twine
- brads
- number and alphabet stickers
- die-cut headline
- computer and printer
- ½-inch circle punch
- paper cutter
- photo markers in blue and orange
- adhesive

Fold over one edge of the cardboard mat.

Tear an opening in the newspaper mat and slip in the photo.

Wrap the photos with twine and knot on the front.

Punch out cardboard circles to back the alphabet stickers.

boo

Make it spook-tacular with a haunted house that provides openings to silhouette trick-or-treaters. To make it, photocopy *pages 327* and *329*; cut out the house. Cut the door opening along the dotted line and back with lime green. The moon, ground paper, and accents also are provided.

Use stitched appliqués found in the notion section of fabric stores to make lettering easy.

Tack strings in place using a dot of thick white crafts glue.

Trim the web to fit in the corner of the page and use the discarded pieces to trim the windows.

Fold open the door to create another photo placement area.

QUICK TIP

Use white colored pencil to create highlights on the left and underside of house features.

materials

- photos
- polka-dot paper or photocopy of papers, page 327 and 329
- solid papers in black, lime green, and yellow
- 12-inch square of lavender background paper
- tracing paper
- pencil
- crafts knife
- white colored pencil
- permanent black marking pen
- scissors
- dimensional spider, web, and pumpkin stickers
- stitched appliqué letters to spell "BOO!"
- thick white crafts glue
- adhesive

see pages 327 and 329

QUICK TIP

Trim the patterned paper slightly and mount on black to reveal a narrow border.

materials

- photo
- 12-inch squares of card stock in black, green, and yellow
- orange paper with black dots
- pumpkin cutouts
- black paper fence
- alphabet punches
- chalk
- foam squares
- adhesive

four little pumpkins

Make it hauntingly happy with black and orange as the primary colors on the page. This fence idea works perfectly for photos taken at a pumpkin patch or during jack-o'-lantern carving.

Use alphabet punches to make a headline quick and easy.

To create dimension mount a photo on card stock using foam squares.

Choose a background paper with a small pattern to add texture without distracting from the photo.

Cut a paper moon to shine beneath the lettering.

got turkey?

Make it funny using photo caption blurbs. To avoid errors write the words on the stickers before placing them on the page.

Cut windows in reversible paper for added interest.

Use photo caption stickers to add a lighthearted touch.

Use a white border to accent photos and headline.

Diagonally clip corner of the photo.

QUICK TIP

To highlight a solid-color die cut, use colored pencil.

materials

- photos
- 2 coordinating 8½×11-inch pieces of reversible paper
- 8½×11-inch piece of white paper
- scissors
- crafts knife
- self-adhesive brown paper leaf shapes
- orange-brown colored pencil
- blank photo caption stickers
- black fine-line permanent marking pen
- metallic gold alphabet stickers
- adhesive

Christmas 2001
Ryan asked the jolly ol' fellow for a magic set and a football. On Morgan's list was a dolly, books, and a kitty (stuffed or real!).

Spread the merry spirit of the season throughout your next holiday scrapbook album.

joy to the world

Detail the plaid strips with metal swirl paper clips.

believe

Make it torn by applying ripped strips of scrapbook paper to accent one side of the photo, the tag, and the headline.

materials

- photo
- 12-inch square of red card stock
- 12-inch square of red and green plaid scrapbook paper
- 12-inch square of black and white type scrapbook paper
- card stock scraps in red and cream
- fabric trim headline
- metal swirl paper clips
- brads
- fibers in red, green, and white
- paper punch
- computer and printer
- paper trimmer
- adhesive

Cut tag shapes, layer, punch a hole in the top, and thread with several fibers.

Fold over the end of the headline fabric and thread through a paper clip. Secure in back.

Tear one edge of scrapbook paper strip and fasten over the photo with brads.

naughty or nice

Make it full of glee by grouping photos of kids with different expressions. To keep the page from becoming monotonous, vary the photo sizes, placing three small ones trailing down to the last large one for impact.

QUICK TIP

Layer mats in holiday colors to add pizzazz to the page.

Use a rubber stamp and embossing gloss gel to create a background that is textured.

Vary photo sizes, angles, and expressions to keep the page full of interest.

Dot the background with a gel pen for subtle color.

Use a gold marking pen and embossing gel for a quick headline.

materials

- photos
- 12-inch square of dark green paper
- paper cutter
- papers in red and gold
- holly rubber stamp
- embossing ink pad or slow-drying green or clear pigment ink pad
- embossing powder in green or clear
- embossing heat tool
- gold marking pen
- green gel pen
- adhesive

christmas with sam

Make it purr-fect using the art from *page 331.* These winter and check designs work well with any playful scrapbook page theme. Use the quaint art to frame headline and journal blocks or as

materials

- photos
- two 12-inch squares of dark red card stock
- red check-print paper
- card stock in black, cream, and dark red
- color photocopy of art, page 331
- paper trimmer
- paper punch
- scissors
- computer and printer
- square punch
- cream fibers
- temporary adhesive
- adhesive spacers, such a Pop Dots
- adhesive

Mount a mitten silhouette on black paper and trim a narrow border.

Print comments on designed journal box by attaching box to paper with temporary adhesive before printing.

Layer punched squares on larger check-print squares.

accents, photo corners, photo mats—whatever your layout calls for. The tag and mitten motifs add a cute touch to a page but can also be used as gift tags.

QUICK TIP

Set squares on point.

Crop two photos the same size and align.

Loop fibers through hole in tag.

Art in back of book!

see page 331

christmas past

Make it sparkle using the symbols of the season—holiday-print paper, festive stickers, a die-cut tree, a stocking, and presents—plus star brads, glistening fibers, and multiple mats in holiday hues. Use

materials

- photos
- 12-inch squares of Christmas paper
- Christmas stickers
- colored card stock
- tree die-cut
- assorted fibers
- star brads
- double-stick tape
- glitter accents
- crafting wire
- eyelet tool
- paper punch
- gold heart eyelet
- stocking die cut
- alphabet punches
- adhesive

Wrap a die-cut tree with decorative fiber and place a star brad at the top.

Stack numbers vertically to indicate the year.

To make the stocking die cut appear as an ornament, punch a hole in the corner and attach a heart eyelet in the hole.

QUICK TIP

To make the punched-out headline shine, apply double-stick tape across the top of the letters and add glitter.

muted colors, such as these, for a vintage tribute. When possible, leave the dates on the photos for a truly authentic representation. Arrange the photos to draw the eye from the left page to the right.

Hold glitter accents in place with double-stick tape.

Use stickers to make decorative corner accents and mat details.

season's greetings

Make it vintage using old photos, notes, and greeting cards. Enhance the look with beaded ribbon and flattened foil cups for a sparkling holiday look. To make the foil accents, flatten out baking cups with your fingers. To scallop the border, cut pieces from the foil circles.

materials

- photos
- 12-inch squares of background paper
- 12-inch square of dark red paper
- silver patterned paper
- bonbon-size foil baking cups in red, pink, silver, and turquoise
- silver Season's Greetings die cut
- clear beaded trim
- ⅛-inch-wide double-stick tape
- metallic silver snowflake stickers
- turquoise paper
- silver alphabet stickers
- vintage Christmas note cards (available in antiques stores, or use reproductions)
- vellum
- paper cutter
- adhesive

Use a silver die-cut headline for a sparkling start.

Enlarge a photo Christmas card for big impact.

Use numeral stickers to identify when a snapshot was taken.

Place beaded trim to hang like icicles.

Use a tape runner to adhere the ribbon portion of the beaded length to the page. Add vintage note cards or Christmas cards under and alongside the photos. If you have a holiday letter available, photocopy it on vellum and attach over an opened note card.

QUICK TIP

Flatten foil baking cups to make metallic circles for the design.

Photocopy a handwritten letter, poem, diary entry, or other item to add to the authenticity.

Include vintage note cards for a nostalgic touch.

Use snowflake stickers to carry out the wintry theme and hold papers in place.

merry christmas, abb

Make it gift-wrapped with pages that fold back to reveal a host of photos. To make the bow, trace the full-size patterns on *page 170* onto tracing paper. Cut out patterns, trace on the back of the bow paper, ar cut out. Adhere the bow and ribbon with foam squares to add dimensio

materials

- photos
- 12-inch foldout scrapbook pages (available at scrapbooking stores)
- 12-inch square of ornament-printed paper
- red paper
- chalk
- foam squares
- scissors and/or crafts knife
- ruler
- paper scrap, tag clip art, or purchased gift tag
- paper raffia
- adhesive

Cut ribbon from paper strips to make the pages appear wrapped.

Shade the edges of a gift tag with chalk.

QUICK TIP

Use raffia to tie the tag to the bow.

Mount the bow with foam squares for dimension.

Choose an ornament-laden paper that resembles holiday gift wrap.

abby continued

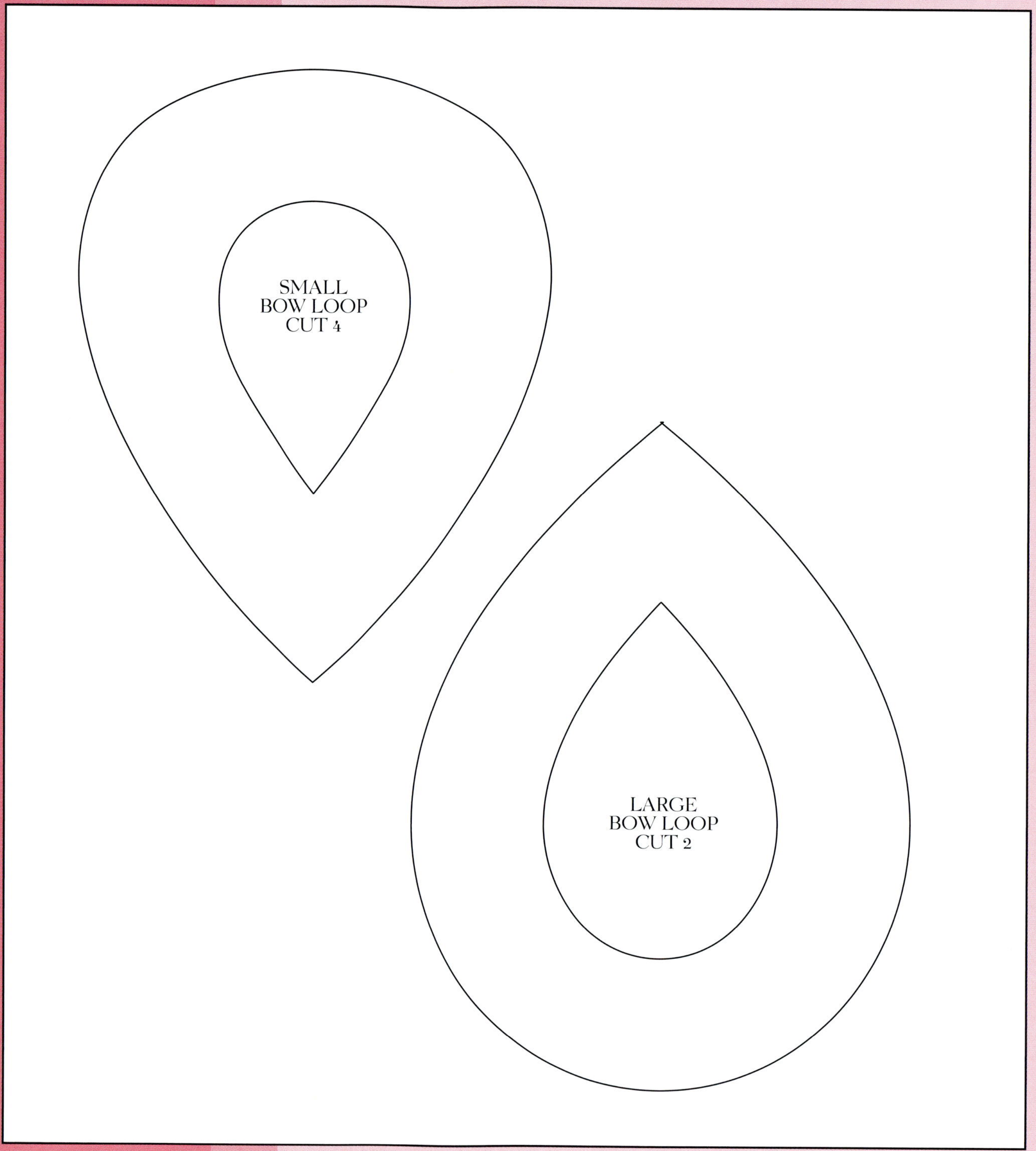

our visit with santa

Make it merry by using the premade art accents on *page 333.* Photocopy and combine the swirl paper, tags, border, and corner triangles to make a magical holiday page.

Accent the page with stars punched from the photocopies and parchment.

Align the journal box with the date.

Center a corner mount at the bottom of the journal box.

Silhouette a figure from a tag to finish off the border strip.

QUICK TIP

Use a punch to create stars from photocopies of holiday art.

materials

- photo
- 12-inch square of red card stock
- color photocopies of holiday art, page 333
- pale yellow parchment
- star punch
- scissors
- computer and printer
- adhesive

Art in back of book!

see page 333

christmas recipe

Make it delicious by including a batch of yummy holiday recipes. Blend those with a handful of favorite photographs, add a pinch of green and red, and include some traditional holiday motifs for a holiday booklet recipe you can complete in an evening. This fun

materials

- photos
- background paper
- mat papers
- scissors
- holiday stickers
- recipes
- fine-line marking pen
- adhesive

Include personal memories about the photos and recipes.

Photocopy recipes, reduced if necessary, to fit a small page format.

combination of ingredients makes it easy to fill the pages, especially when the pages are small. With a white background, the photos, mats, and stickers are all that's needed to make each page interesting.

QUICK TIP

Use postcard-size albums—they also make great gifts.

Holiday stickers add an instant merry touch.

Make your pages any size desired.

Whatever you like to do for fun, these creative, on-the-go pages sing of adventure.

pack your bags

idaho snow

Make it majestic by featuring one color of solid card stock and the exclusive art elements from *pages 335* and *337*. Use the art strips to frame the spread with bold, beautiful color and design. Within the

materials

- photos
- two 12-inch squares of lavender card stock
- card stock in red and white
- color photocopy of art, pages 335 and 337
- alphabet stickers
- marking pens in white and black
- scissors
- paper trimmer
- adhesive

see pages 335 and 337

Position the photocopies of the animals to face into the pages.

Create a snowball out of white card stock, accenting with white marking pen lines.

Handwrite simple journaling: a subhead and a record of names.

frame use a mix of cropped and silhouetted photos and art for a classy combination. These pages use lavender behind the photos, but choose any color to complement your pictures.

QUICK TIP

Use decorative-edge scissors to cut quick zigzag borders.

Apply alphabet stickers to contrasting card stock to create the headline.

Use a different snowflake design in each corner.

sea island

Make it color-coordinated by choosing a single-color scheme. Base the focus color on the main color in your photos; then choose coordinating card stock in at least three shades of that color—light, medium, and dark. Arrange the elements on the page to frame,

materials

- photos
- two 12-inch squares of dark green card stock
- card stock in two lighter shades of green
- computer and printer
- square punch
- paper cutter
- adhesive

Use the darker colors for the background and the lightest for the headline and journaling.

Mat a photo as part of the headline design.

Highlight journaling by adhering punched dots.

overlap, and accent. Use the lightest color in the group for computer-generated journaling. Note how the text is flush right to create organization on the right-hand page.

QUICK TIP

Use punches to balance offset type.

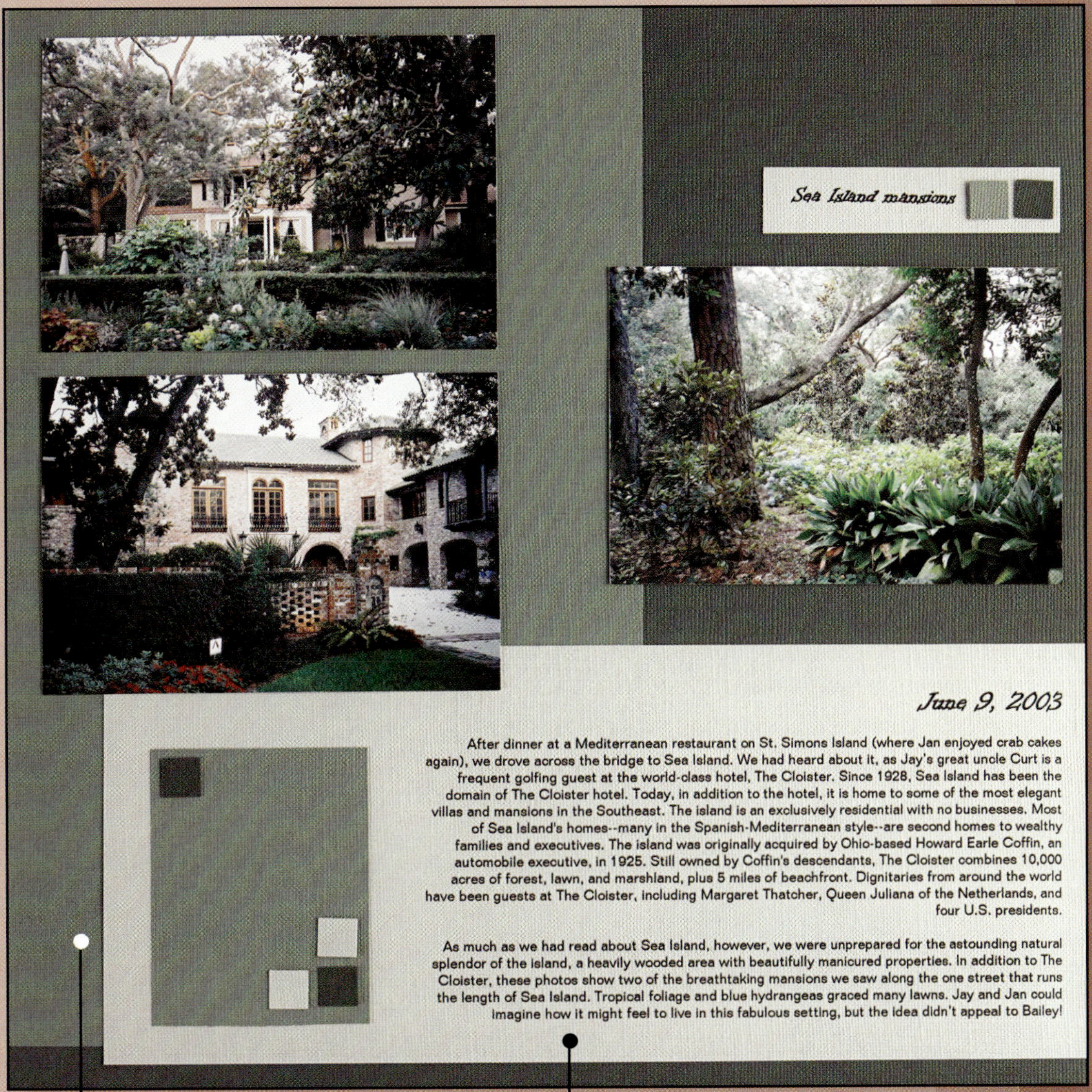

Cut a piece of the medium color lengthwise; then place part of it on each page as the layout center color.

Print journaling and headline on light card stock and mount.

camping

Make it mottled by using rubber stamps to create a subtle or contrasting pattern in the background. Change the color of the ink to connect an endless array of designs. Choose a rubber stamp and ink

materials

- photos
- two 12-inch squares of dark green card stock
- medium green card stock
- vellum
- circle brads
- computer and printer
- paper trimmer
- adhesive

Print the headline and journaling on vellum to allow the background colors to show through.

Mat only the photo that is placed above the headline.

Stamp a background paper with slightly darker ink for a subtle design.

color to complement your layout theme. To make die cuts, stamp card stock and trim around the stamp shape.

QUICK TIP

Use eyelets to attach vellum and to accent the page.

Wrap card stock blocks with fiber; tape the ends to the back of the card stock.

For a spread, cut a sheet of card stock in half and place the halves to appear as mirror images.

Type and print journaling in columns, leaving a space for stickers.

gino's

Make it tasteful with alphabet stickers to make an instant headline. Place the stickers on the background paper or the journal box or to change the look, place only some of the letters on card stock, as shown at *left*.

materials

- photos
- restaurant menu
- 12-inch square of black card stock
- white card stock
- paper trimmer
- adhesive

Embellish the page with decorative stickers that carry out the theme.

Tear and chalk the bottom of the journal block.

Whip up an artistic headline by placing a couple of the alphabet stickers on small rectangles of card stock.

Mat photos to separate them from the print background.

black hills railroad

Make it roll right along using color-block printed paper. This type of paper has such details as the headline area, photo mats, and tags printed on the paper. Rotate the background paper to suit your page.

QUICK TIP

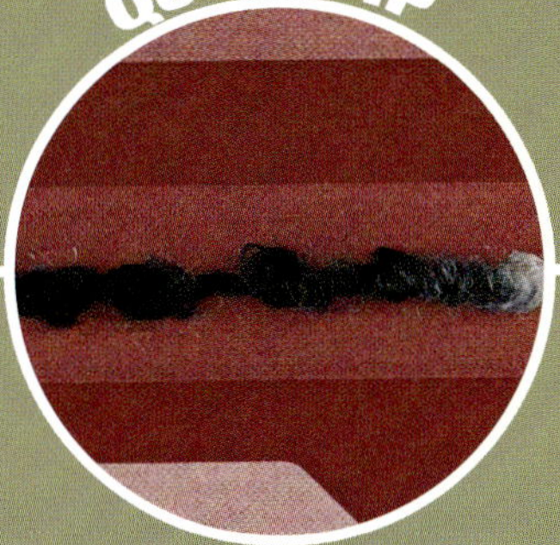

Make the preprinted blocks look more dimensional using fiber and eyelets.

Thread fiber through eyelets; tape the ends on the page back.

Cut a scenic photo into thirds and place on tags. Punch a hole in the top of each tag and secure eyelets in the holes.

Use the measuring guides on the back of the background paper to create the headline and journaling strip.

materials

- photos
- 12-inch square of color-block paper
- card stock in white and black
- black brads
- silver eyelets and eyelet tool
- fibers in white, gray, and black
- paper punch
- computer and printer
- paper trimmer
- adhesive
- tape

field museum

Make it punchy using punches and paper scraps. Punches are often overlooked in favor of more trendy tools and embellishments. But punches, especially simple geometric shapes, enable you to create

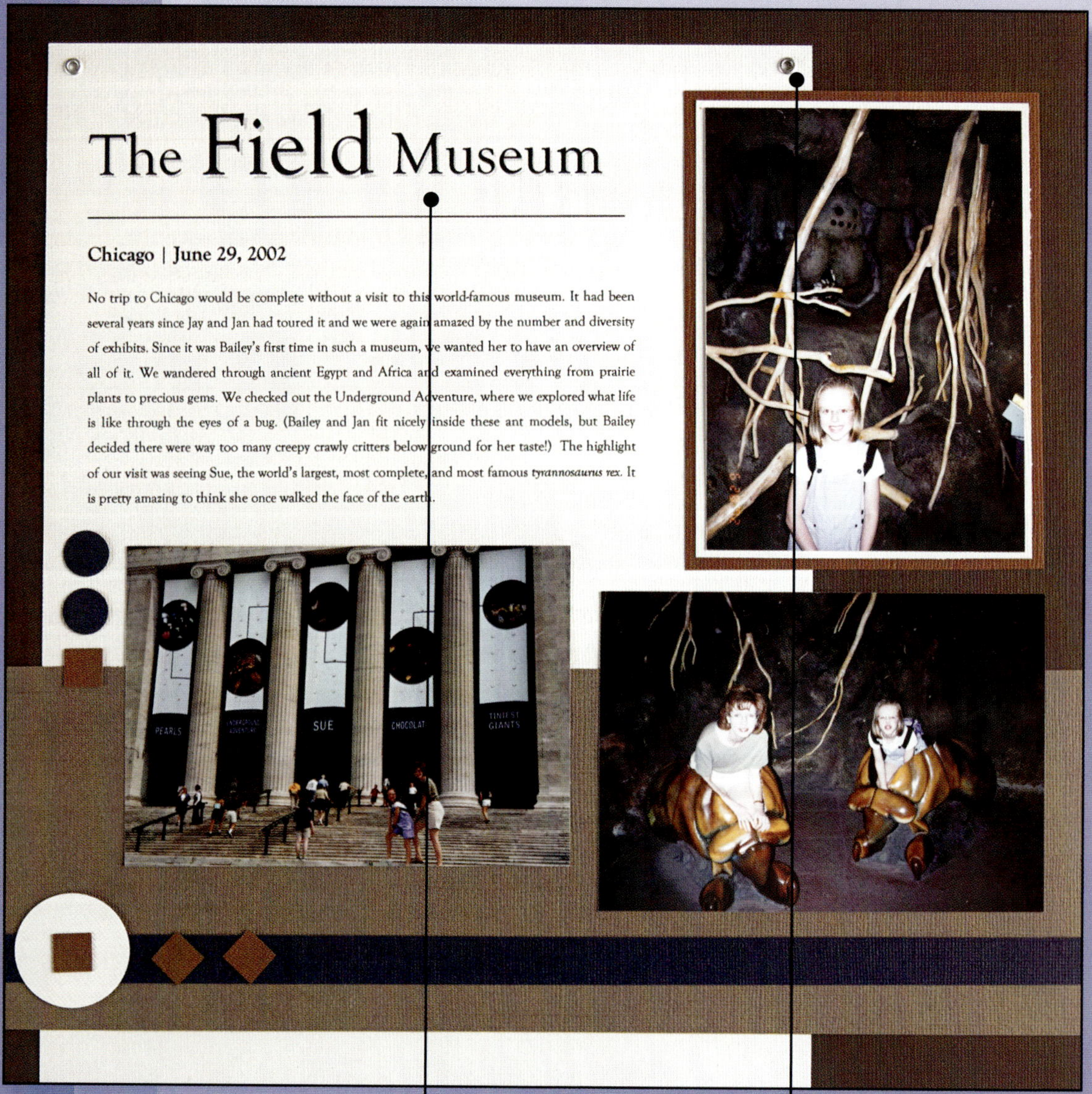

materials

- photos
- two 12-inch squares of dark brown card stock
- card stock in white, beige, rust, and royal blue
- punches in circle and square shapes
- eyelets
- fiber
- paper trimmer
- computer and printer
- adhesive

Print headline and journaling on a large piece of card stock that doubles as a photo mat.

Secure journaling to layout with eyelets.

simple, timeless designs in no time flat. In this layout a combination of circle and square punches lends stylish flair.

Punch a variety of circles and squares and arrange along the border strip of each page.

Mat only the two principal photos.

QUICK TIP

Keep memorabilia that may contain acid away from photos using eyelet and fiber accents.

QUICK TIP

Draw the eye from start to finish using square punches and brads.

jekyll island

Make it clean with a single-photo layout. This serene design gives you an opportunity to include a special poem, quotation, or journaling to convey your thoughts. Strong lines and monochromatic colors allow the photo and journaling to be prominent.

materials

- photo
- 12-inch square of black card stock
- card stock in black and light gray, and medium gray
- eyelet and eyelet tool
- square punch
- square brads
- computer and printer
- paper trimmer
- adhesive

Adhere coordinating card stock strips to the background, leaving narrow borders.

Select a special photo to mat or frame.

Print journaling, ragged left, in the appropriate position on a 9x8½-inch card stock rectangle.

Insert an eyelet in one corner of the frame.

on the road

Make it in a snap by cropping photos to fit in a grid pattern. Choose a solid-color background paper that contrasts with the photos to eliminate the need for matting. The patterns for the car border are on *page 277.*

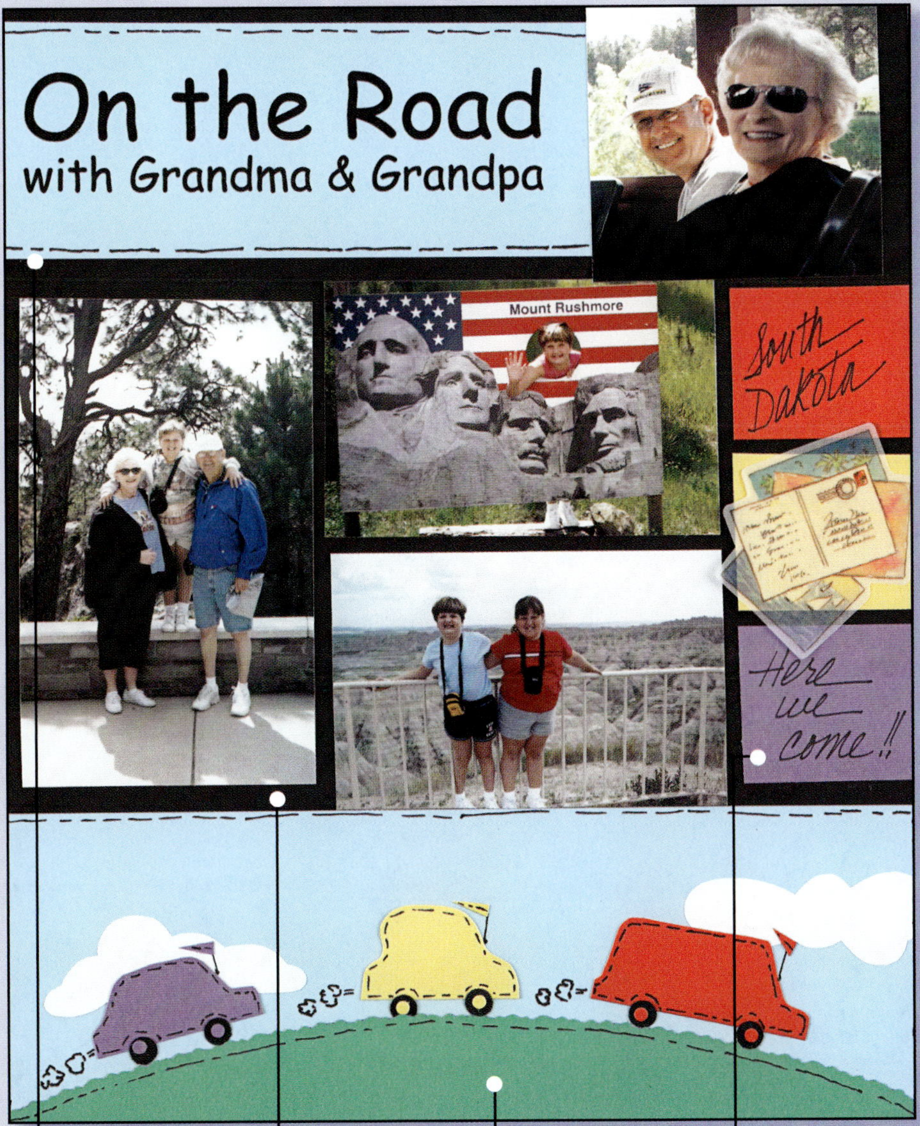

Print the headline and draw a broken-line border.

Leave narrow borders between the photos.

Anchor the page with the car border, using the pattern on page 277 and card stock.

Run the headline and card stock blocks off the page.

Use the edge of an index card to guide straight writing.

materials

- photos
- 8½×11-inch black card stock
- card stock in light blue, red, yellow, green, white, and purple
- photocopy of car patterns, page 277
- vellum postcard sticker
- black fine-line marking pen
- computer and printer
- scissors
- paper trimmer
- adhesive

see page 277

Print a headline on vellum to allow the background to show through.

fun at the lake

Make it without extra papers using several photos without mats. Leave space near the center of the photo grouping to create a scene made with stickers. For the sun pattern, see *page 277.*

Use stickers to reinforce the theme. Attach vellum to the background using stickers.

Crop photos to fill the lower half of the page, allowing narrow borders.

Use the sun pattern to draw a sun on a strip of card stock. Color in the sun and rays with colored pencils. Cut and color a strip for water if desired. Print the headline on vellum and adhere in the open area.

materials

- photos
- 12-inch square of white card stock
- vellum
- photocopy of sun pattern, page 277
- beach-theme stickers
- colored pencils
- computer and printer
- scissors
- paper trimmer
- adhesive

see page 277

our day at the mall

Make it bouncy using colorful paper circles and squares to back photos and increase contrast on the page. To crop circles in seconds, use a circle cutter. A paper trimmer makes squares, rectangles, and strips in just a couple of quick slices.

QUICK TIP

Use conversation blurb stickers in place of journaling.

Print the headline and subheads on white paper and cut them into strips.

Use a circle cutter to make circles in a jiffy.

Position a white card stock circle over the end of the headline box to make a unit.

materials

- photos
- 12-inch square of black card stock
- card stock in white, red, yellow, turquoise, and blue
- white paper
- conversation blurb stickers
- paper trimmer
- computer and printer
- circle cutter
- adhesive

Choose subtle-print card stocks that create texture without looking busy.

riding the waves

Make it splash without using any embellishments. Mount some of the photos on colorful card stock. Then arrange them and a pair of paper strips around the headline.

materials

- photos
- 12-inch square of blue striped card stock
- subtle-pattern card stock in red and yellow
- vellum
- paper trimmer
- computer and printer
- tape
- adhesive

Print journaling on vellum and place on top of a photo.

Double-mount the main photo.

Print the headline words on yellow card stock and trim leaving wide borders. Tear holes in the blue background paper and tape the headline underneath it.

skiing

Make it circular using circle and oval cutters. Crop several photos with these tools, place the photos on a theme-print background paper, and you're almost done.

QUICK TIP

Use different sizes of the same font to print the headline and journaling boxes.

Arrange photos on page to leave room for the headline and labels.

Group photos of the same person to share one label.

Mount a sticker on card stock and edge with a broken line using a marking pen.

materials

- photos
- 12-inch square of theme-print paper
- card stock in yellow and white
- water-theme sticker
- blue fine-line marking pen
- circle cutter
- oval cutter
- scissors
- adhesive

QUICK TIP

Highlight special items from photos by silhouetting them and placing them in corners.

materials

- photos
- 12-inch square of brown card stock
- tan card stock
- scrap of brown card stock
- eyelets and eyelet tool
- shell stickers
- paper trimmer
- computer and printer
- brown chalk
- scissors
- adhesive
- adhesive spacers, such as Pop Dots

tidelands

Make it geometric by color-blocking to organize pages quickly and easily. Skip the photo mats and arrange photos and card stock pieces in a blocked design for a stylized scrapbook page.

Group theme-related stickers on a card stock rectangle, raising one or two of the stickers from the background using adhesive spacers.

Accent card stock pieces with eyelets.

shedd aquarium

Make it documented using a travel brochure to accent the page and to remember details from a trip. Attach it to the page with a paper strip embellished with punched squares and string.

QUICK TIP

Hold a brochure in place with rubber cement.

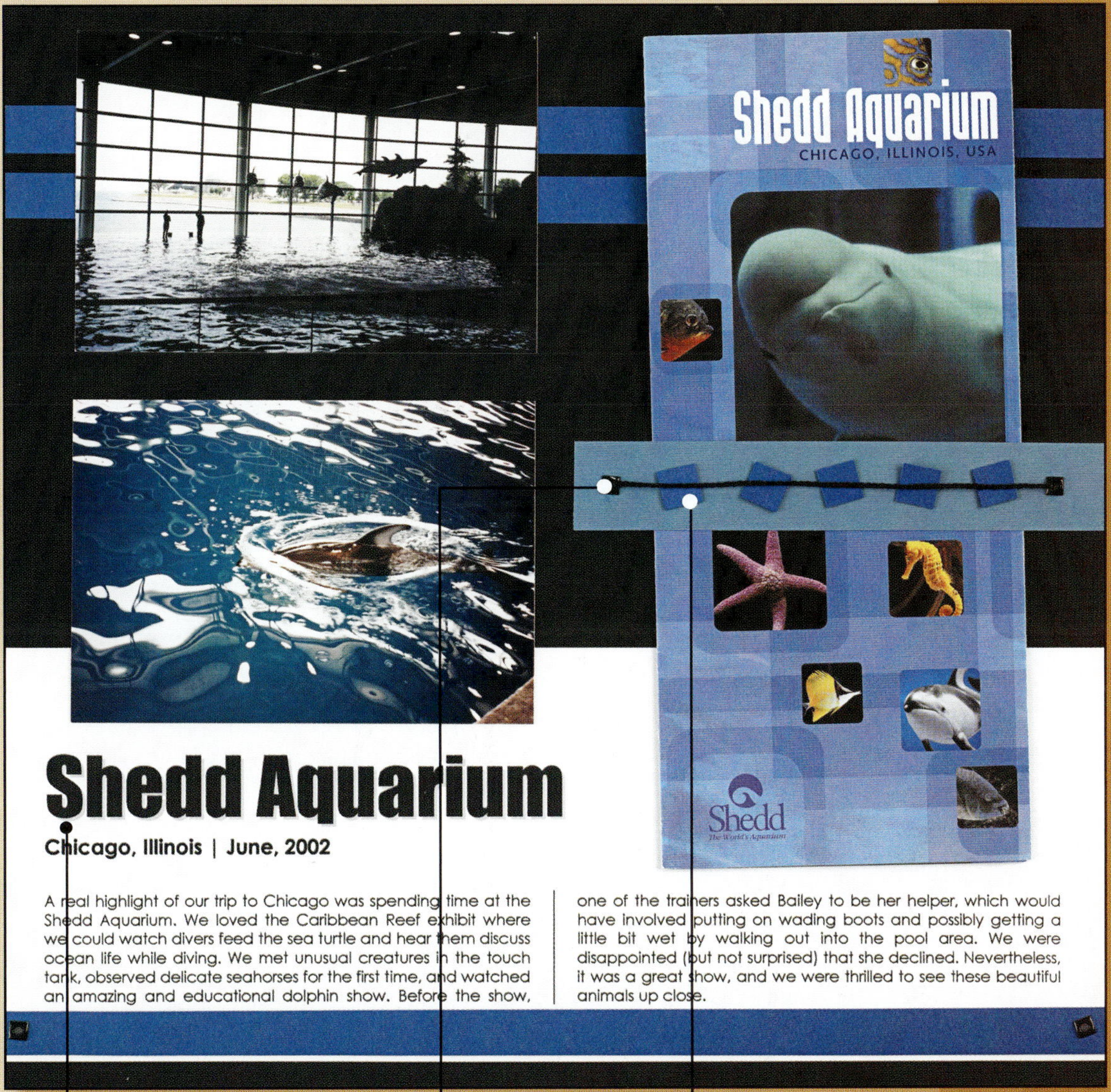

Position the headline at the top of a two-column journal box.

Tape string ends on the back of the background card stock.

Glue punched squares along a paper strip and attach an eyelet at each end.

materials

- photos
- 12-inch square of black card stock
- 4¼×12-inch rectangle of white card stock
- card stock in royal and light blue
- brochure
- square black eyelets and eyelet tool
- black string
- square punch
- computer and printer
- paper trimmer
- adhesive
- rubber cement

QUICK TIP

Combine fibers and raffia to create a natural look.

sod house

Make it printed by computer-generating the title and journaling to start off this historic page. To create an aged look, darken the edges of the papers with brown chalk. Tear and chalk the edges of the photo mats to contribute character and a vintage look to the page.

materials

- photos
- 12-inch squares of light sage green and dark sage green card stock
- tan card stock scraps
- nature-theme paper cutout
- raffia
- brown chenille string
- eyelets
- eyelet tool
- brown chalk
- computer and printer
- iron
- paper trimmer
- adhesive
- tape

Combine two types of fibers—paper raffia and soft chenille string. Tape raffia ends to the back of the page.

Wet, crinkle, and iron card stock to make a textured background paper.

Tear paper edges and rub them with brown chalk.

snow much fun

Make it headline-centered with a collection of photos placed around the words. Using stickers apply the headline to white paper and trim for added emphasis. Crop some of the photos rectangular and others round to provide variety and create symmetry.

QUICK TIP

Use stickers to make borders quick as a wink.

materials

- photos
- card stock in blue and white
- stickers
- white opaque marking pen
- adhesive

Use an opaque marking pen to draw snowflakes and to journal.

Crop the photos round to add variety to the page shapes.

Mount a sticker on white card stock and trim around it to stand out on the page.

Choose medium blue paper to provide a neutral background for wintry photos.

the badlands

Make it overlapped using blocks of solid-color card stock to make a background for scenic photos. For the quickest method, use a paper trimmer or purchased precut pieces of card stock. Choose two

materials

- photos
- two 12-inch squares of cream card stock
- card stock in rust, olive, and tan
- cream vellum
- alphabet die-cut machine
- eyelets and eyelet tool
- paper trimmer
- adhesive

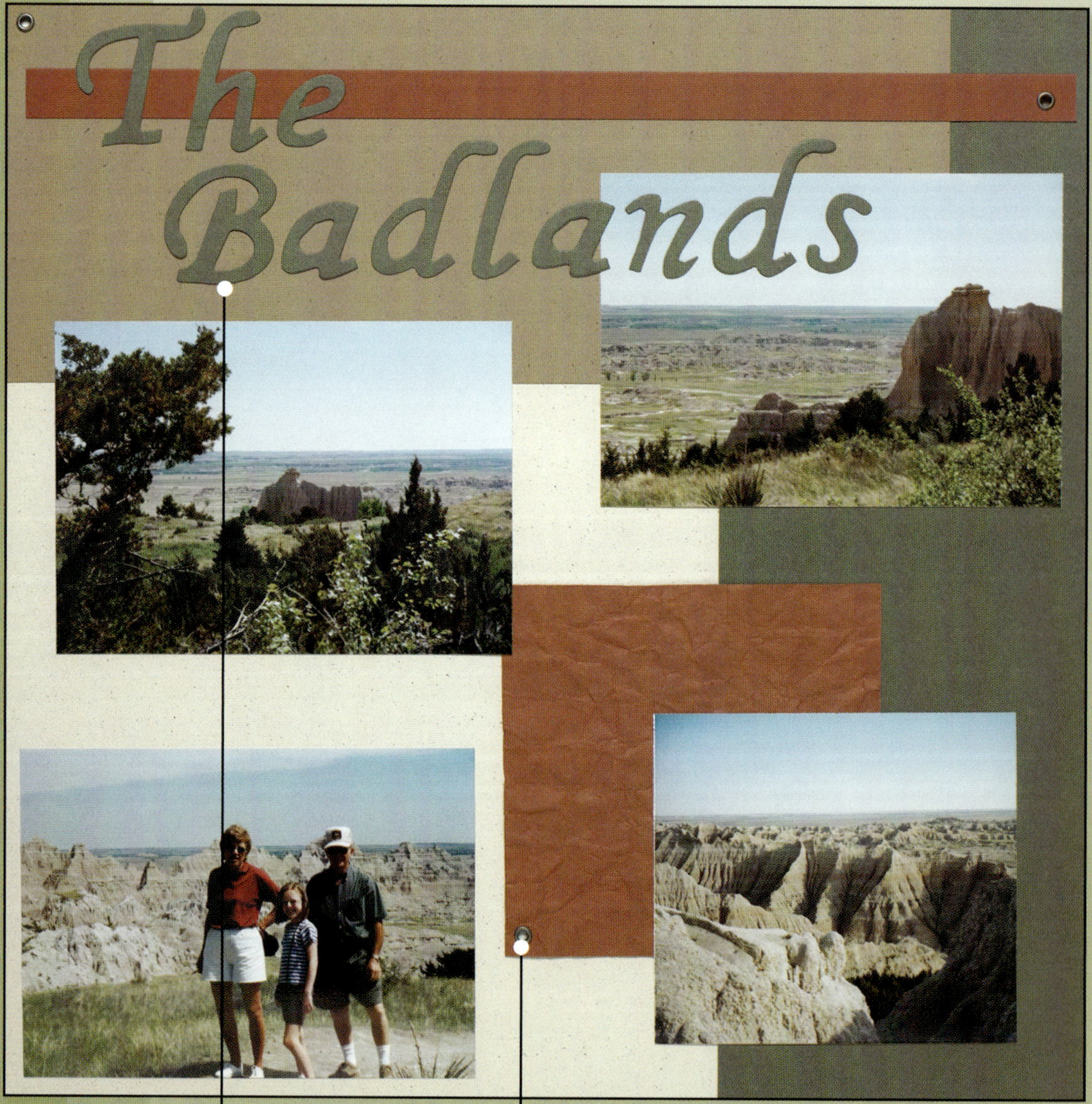

Create a bold headline from coordinating card stock using a die-cut machine.

Use eyelets to produce artistic details on the card stock.

QUICK TIP

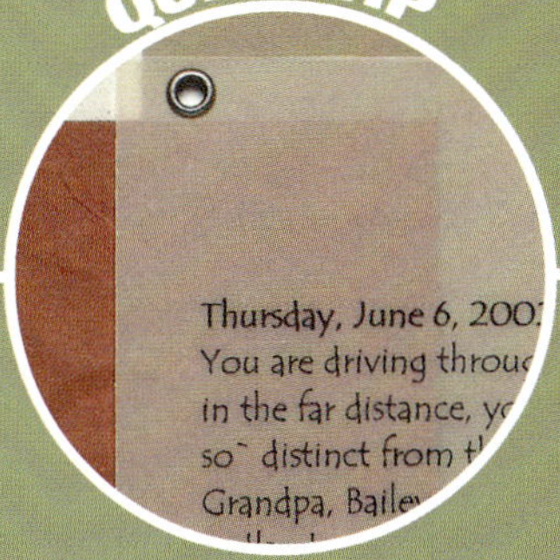

Print type on vellum to allow the background to show through subtly.

or three colors to unify the pages and to minimize cost. To allow the background to show through in a subtle manner, print journaling on vellum. Use long paper strips to anchor the pages.

Overlap card stock squares and rectangles to create a layered look. These card stock shapes are often available as precut pieces.

the best day

Make it stand out using large photographs that display drama. Crop one photo horizontally the width of the page. Silhouette another photo that has an interesting shape. Mat the remaining photos for

materials

- photos
- 12-inch square of orange card stock
- 12-inch square of bright blue card stock
- card stock scraps in orange, green, red, and yellow
- black permanent marking pen
- scissors
- paper trimmer
- adhesive

Makes notes of your child's comments and use them to journal.

Silhouette a large shape to give the page a focus.

the opposite page and place on smaller blocks of color. Overlap photos slightly to keep the layout from becoming too busy.

QUICK TIP

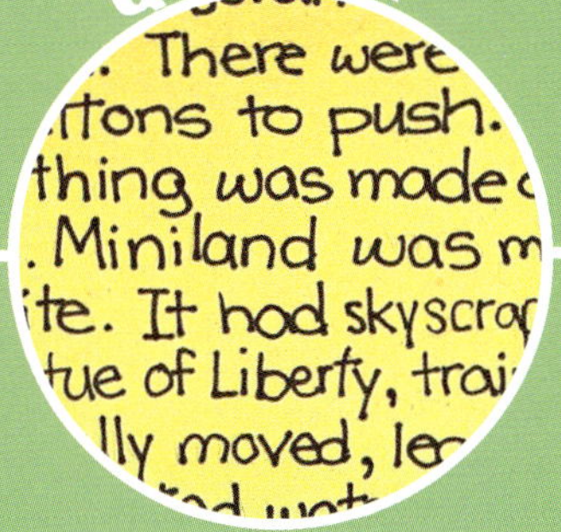

Use a disappearing-ink pen to draw guides for handprinted journaling.

Jazz up the page using single and layered card stock rectangles.

de smet

Make it lickety-split with a paper trimmer or purchased precut pieces of card stock. Choosing only two or three colors helps unify the pages. Punch out the headline letters and lap them over two

materials

- photos
- two 12-inch squares of medium green card stock
- 12-inch squares of card stock in dark green and white
- 8½×11-inch rectangles of card stock in tan and light green
- scrap of black card stock
- alphabet die-cut machine or die-cut letters for headline
- square punch
- paper punch
- 3 black brads
- paper trimmer
- computer and printer
- adhesive

Leave space at the top of the journal box for the headline.

Punch out squares from card stock and glue in pairs.

paper colors to integrate them. Punch out squares to use as page accents, grouping in pairs. Tilt tag shapes to use as journaling boxes. Top off the tags with paper rectangles and brads.

QUICK TIP

Adhere the same color of card stock strips across two pages.

Attach small card stock rectangles with brads.

Make a tag shape by clipping off two corners of a rectangle.

hawaii band trip

Make it tropical using mirror-image art elements available on *pages 339* and *341.* The tree and wave designs coordinate with any sea theme. With the additions of the sun and floral motifs, all these pages need are photos!

materials

- photos
- two 12-inch squares of gold card stock
- 12-inch square of plum card stock
- scrap of pink card stock
- photocopy of art, pages 339 and 341
- white alphabet stickers
- scissors
- paper trimmer
- permanent marking pens
- adhesive

see page 339 and 341

Layer the decorative frame, matted photo, and flower cutout.

Enlarge wave art on page 339 to 110 percent to extend the width of the paper.

Color in white alphabet stickers to create a bold headline.

Make a mirror-image copy of the wave for the right page.

Color in the alphabet stickers to coordinate with the page colors.

Silhouette a flower from the photo mat for a corner accent.

summer storm

Make it somber by accenting the page with monochromatic squares and stripes. Tie two pages together by placing narrow horizontal stripes across the spread. Use the same colors to mat two photos as

materials

- photos
- two 12-inch squares of navy blue card stock
- 12-inch squares of card stock in light and medium blue-gray
- scraps of navy blue card stock
- paper trimmer
- computer and printer
- date stamp
- adhesive

Balance the pages by placing square designs in opposite corners of spread.

Mat only the focal point photos.

well as the headline and corner motifs. Print out the journaling in blocks to maintain the block design.

QUICK TIP

Cut a square diagonally to create two triangles.

Place the title on the right-hand page for interest.

Stylize the background using monochromatic strips of card stock.

QUICK TIP

Print a black background and reverse lettering on scrapbook paper.

materials

- **2 enlarged photos, one vertical and one to silhouette shapes**
- **12-inch square of coordinating print scrapbook paper**
- **$8\frac{1}{2}\times11$-inch scrapbook paper to fit in printer**
- **tan paper**
- **scissors**
- **paper trimmer**
- **computer and printer**
- **adhesive**

whatsa buckeye?

Make it magnified using enlarged photos. Pick a vertical shot to run the full length of the page. For accents enlarge and silhouette elements from a related photo, such as the buckeyes at the page bottom.

Silhouette elements from one of the enlargements.

Place the vertical photo left of center.

Use a dictionary-style definition to explain a theme.

link to the past

Make it a detailed record by printing the subhead and journaling on the background paper. For variety, print at the bottom of the page, breaking the type into two columns. This leaves room for photos at the top.

QUICK TIP

Cut out a sign from a photo to create a headline.

Mount two of the photos on card stock and trim narrow borders.

Chalk the edges of the mat papers.

Group the silhouetted headline and the leaf die cut.

materials

- photos
- 12-inch square of dark brown card stock
- card stock in light and medium brown
- leaf die cut
- eyelets and eyelet tool
- computer and printer
- brown chalk
- paper trimmer
- adhesive

morocco in june

Make it enlivened with special touches, such as rounding the photo corners and matting them with colored paper, using large headlines, placing journaling in blocks, and tying fibers in knots. When you

materials

- photos
- two 12-inch squares of tan background paper
- sunburst yellow card stock
- deckle-edge decorative scissors
- corner rounder
- sunburst template
- lettering template
- computer and printer
- fiber
- yellow eyelets
- eyelet tool
- paper punch
- light orange decorating chalks
- alphabet template
- crafts glue
- adhesive

Knot fibers for a natural touch to your vacation spread.

Use alphabet templates to make headlines that coordinate.

Use one decorative-edge pair of scissors for continuity.

have several photos to display, these simple embellishments will add punch without distracting from the main focus.

QUICK TIP

Punch a hole in paper before adding eyelet.

Cut the sunburst in half and apply each half to facing pages, aligning the straight edges.

Use orange chalk to shadow the sunburst rays.

Use a template to make paper shapes to fit the theme.

Use computer-generated journaling to help simplify the page.

Use a paper punch as a starter hole to cut out openings in letters.

spain

Make it stunning using a headline crafted from a photo. If necessary enlarge the photo. To make the pattern, choose a chunky computer fon and print using the mirror image setting. Use spray adhesive to adhere the pattern to the photo back and cut out the letters.

materials

- photos
- 12-inch square of black background paper
- paper that complements the headline photo
- computer and printer
- paper trimmer
- crafts knife
- paper punch
- spray adhesive
- adhesive

Extend the letters to the top and side edges of the background paper.

Use a paper color that enhances the headline photo.

Silhouette a snapshot of a person and glue it over a scenic photo.

Use bold type and a striking photo to create the headline.

iceland

Make it in shades, such as the grays used with these black and white photographs. If you want to create this look and your photos are in color, take them to a copy shop and have them output in black and white on photographic paper.

QUICK TIP

Trim a caption with an arrow at one end to signify direction.

Use a panoramic shot to set the mood for a vacation spread.

Turn papers on point to make a design element.

Choose a geometric background to unify a graphic layout.

materials

- photos
- 12-inch square of background paper
- parchment, vellum, and other papers in shades of gray
- computer and printer
- crafts knife
- adhesive

st. michael's

Make it angelic using sky background to honor a church or other religious theme. Choose papers that relate to the location, keeping in mind that the background paper should enhance, not overpower,

materials

- photos
- two 12-inch squares of background paper
- paper cutter
- neutral paper for photo mounting
- computer and printer
- black fine-line marking pen
- adhesive

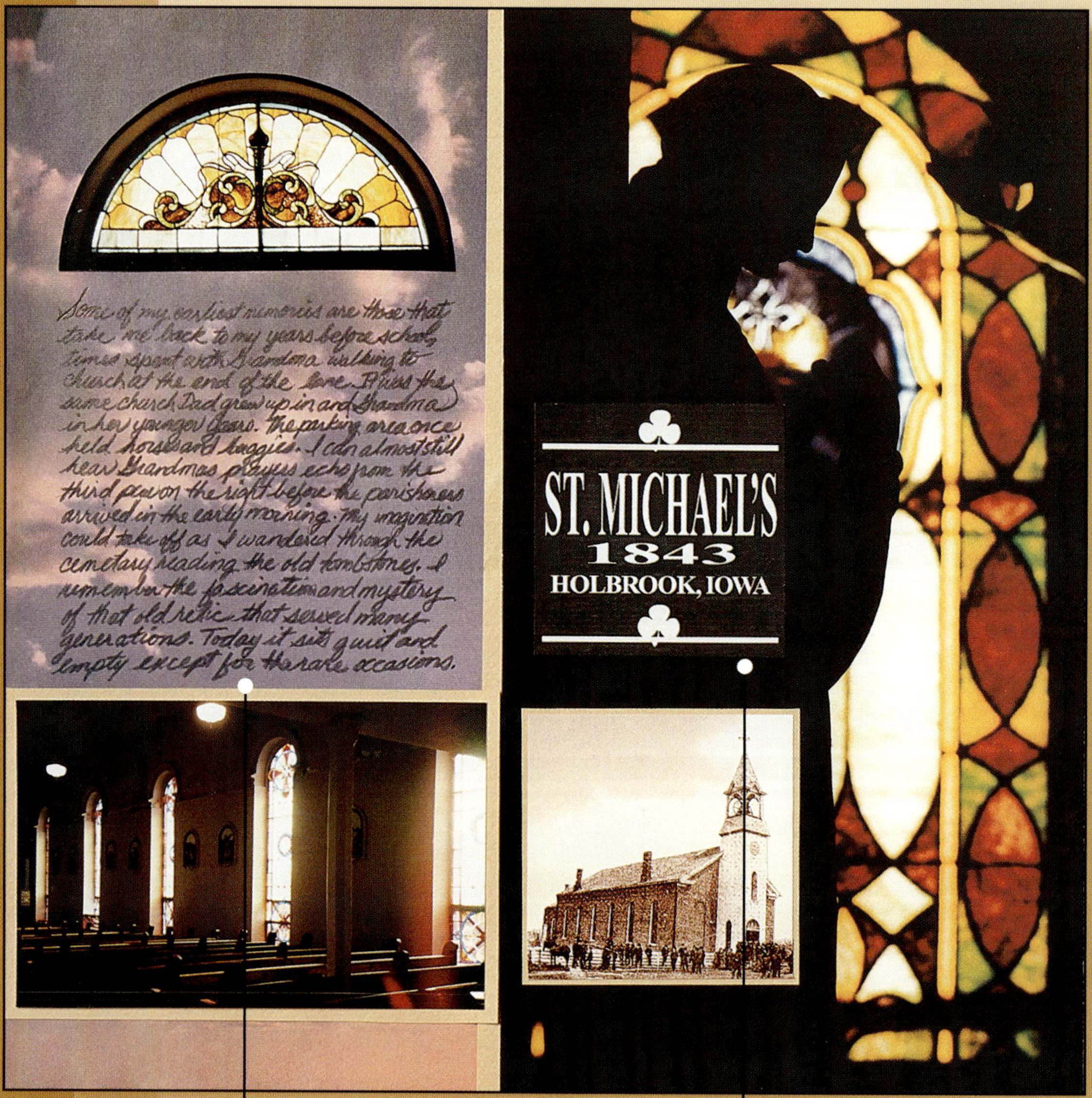

Handwrite personal memories in a block.

Use large voids in photos to inset headlines and small photos.

QUICK TIP

Allow a photo to extend to the background edges for extra impact.

the photos. When photos include a lot of color, mount them on neutral papers before adhering them to the background.

Include photos of architectural details.

Photograph artifacts that have special meaning to you.

sand castles

Make it sun-kissed with watercolor scrapbook paper that provides the perfect background to enhance beach photos. For interest show a mix of people, birds or animals, and seashells that tell the story.

materials

- photos
- two 12-inch squares of watercolor background paper
- crafts knife
- scissors
- ruler
- white opaque marker
- seashells
- glue pen
- white glitter
- adhesive

Add dimension by using small, fairly flat seashells.

Choose a watercolor background paper with smooth warm/cool blended colors to carry out the beach theme.

Use a white opaque marking pen to create freestyle curved writing.

QUICK TIP

When silhouetting small images, move the photo instead of the scissors for a clean cut.

Take the photos from a variety of distances to give the pages a push-pull appearance.

Retrace the journaling with a glue pen and sprinkle it with glitter.

Use several face sizes to provide interest and variety.

las vegas

Make it a winner by celebrating friendship and fun with a spread devoted to both. Whether you take a vacation with a friend or enjoy a special outing, capture it in photos to treasure always. Because the

materials

- photos
- computer and printer
- colored pencils in yellow, yellow-orange, and orange
- two 12-inch squares of white background paper
- 12-inch square of map-print paper
- two 12-inch squares of cloud-patterned vellum paper
- 12-inch squares of American money printed paper
- press-on gems
- border line stickers
- die-cut Eiffel Tower
- vacation mementos, such as show ticket stubs and 3-D glasses
- scissors
- adhesive

Use colored pencils to color in a computer-generated letter outlines.

Overlay map paper with cloud vellum to subtly screen it.

Use cloud-patterned vellum to create a soft background for your photos.

theme of this vacation is Las Vegas, money paper is a playful choice. Select papers that coordinate with your own travel location.

QUICK TIP

To cover a paper edge and to create a horizon line, adhere a border line sticker.

Apply press-on gems to make sparkling accents.

Use vacation mementos to personalize the page.

Frame captions in black.

Press on a border line sticker for a horizon line.

sabbatical

Make it roar using only the best photos from a collection in a large manner. Separate legs of the trip with headlines using a look that fits the region. Set apart the main headline in a block of copy created on a computer. To make a pattern for each of the headlines, choose

materials

- two 12-inch squares of blue background paper
- papers for borders and headlines
- paper cutter
- crafts knife
- computer and printer
- beige paper for printer
- red marker
- adhesive

Generate headlines on a computer, print backward, adhere to colored paper, and trim out.

Inset photos in open spaces of larger photos.

Enlarge candid photos for a dramatic effect.

QUICK TIP

Turn captions around corners for interest.

bold, chunky computer fonts. Print each word in reverse (mirror image or flipped horizontally). Using spray adhesive adhere the desired color paper to the back of the printed word. Cut out the letters and adhere to the background paper or to contrasting paper.

Create a journaling focal point, such as this S, by using an outline computer font with a shadow. Color in the letter with a marking pen.

Balance the overall color in the layout by placing identical colors across the spread.

norway

Make it reflect the destination using items that speak of the locale. Because knitted items were some of these vacationers' favorite finds, one of the scarves they purchased during their trip was photocopied

materials

- photos
- 12-inch squares of black card stock
- mats to coordinate with photos
- paper cutter
- computer and printer
- opaque white marking pen
- adhesive

Photograph a favorite purchase for added memories.

Select photo mats to coordinate with photos.

and used on the page. The label was included to record the manufacturer. Keep this technique in mind to include stores, places, or other information in your design.

QUICK TIP

Tuck labels under the framed photos for informal journaling.

Use a computer to make journaling a breeze.

Save a piece of currency to include on pages devoted to travels abroad.

An opaque marking pen stands out on a deep red tone.

america the beautiful

Make it all-American with a background of amber waves of grain using the papers on *pages 343* and *345.* To cover a 12-inch-square page, enlarge the background paper on *page 343* 111 percent on a photocopier. The mat bars, star boxes, and journaling box are full-size.

materials

- photos
- papers or photocopies of exclusive papers, pages 343 and 345
- blue paper
- scissors
- crafts knife
- ruler
- adhesive

Overlap photos, being careful to cover up only uninteresting areas.

Use star art for photo corners and as accents.

Place the headlines at slight angles as though made from a fabric banner.

Use solid papers to mount some of the photos to prevent the layout from becoming too busy.

The side bars are mirror images. To achieve this, photocopy one bar from *page 345* at 111 percent, then copy a second bar using a mirror or flip setting on the copier. To make the photo mats, photocopy several stripes; cut out. Glue star squares to cover the corner seams.

This leaf and grain paper is available on page 343.

Make a reversed photocopy of the side banner for a mirror image.

see pages 343 and 345

Pay tribute to Mother Nature with scrapbook pages that win naturally.

the great outdoors

gardening

Make it picturesque by dividing the page with wide horizontal and narrow vertical strips. This approach separates the pages into a grid, facilitating beautiful and quick organization. Alternate the photo

materials

- photos
- two 12-inch squares each of dark olive and light olive card stock
- two ¼×12-inch strips of plum card stock
- scraps of card stock in pink, mauve, plum, medium olive, and rust
- flower punches in large and small sizes
- circle punches in large and small sizes
- computer and printer
- adhesive
- glue dots

Punch flowers from card stock and adhere to background with glue dots.

Adhere flower centers with glue stick.

Cut freehand stems and leaves.

position from top to bottom to maintain a welcome page flow. Add leaf and flower punch accents, and you've got a design that's blooming with creativity.

QUICK TIP

Use vertical strips to divide photos and horizontal strips to mat photos and text.

Balance the headline block with journal blocks.

Devote each grid unit to photos, punched flowers, or journaling.

dad's garden

Make it breathtaking using a painterly backdrop for brilliant floral photographs. The green background paper accentuates the color in gorgeous outdoor photos. To soften the look of each photo,

materials

- photos
- 12-inch squares of background paper
- paper cutter
- corner rounder
- colored papers for borders
- green marking pen
- yellow tube-style paint
- decorative-edge scissors
- adhesive

Use decorative-edge scissors to cut strips of color for emphasis.

Cover dead space in a photograph with a small interesting inset.

Create a focal point using one large vertical photo with double matting.

use a corner rounder. To spice up large uninteresting areas in photos, add a photo inset, such as the orange poppies at the bottom of the large vertical photo.

QUICK TIP

Coordinate mat colors with an element from the photo.

Round the photo corners for a delicate look.

Use green journaling for legibility without distracting from the colorful photos.

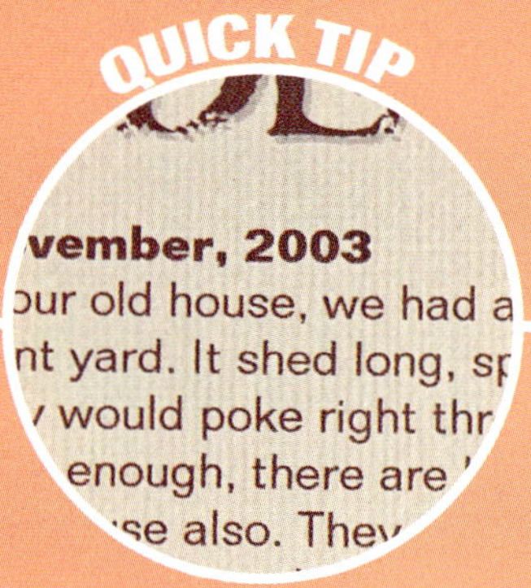

Print journaling on light color 8½×11-inch paper; overlap with card stock.

ode to the pods

Make it in minutes with a color-blocked card stock background. Choose three or four colors that coordinate with your photos and cut the card stock into squares and rectangles. For a more textural look tear the edges.

materials

- photos
- 12-inch square of dark brown card stock
- card stock scraps to coordinate with photos
- 8½×11-inch piece of light-color paper
- leaf die cut
- brads
- paper punch
- paper trimmer
- computer and printer
- adhesive

Adhere a die cut to a small piece of card stock.

Plan journaling in blocks at the top and bottom of the page. Use an ink color complementary to the card stock.

Place some blocks to run to the edge of the page.

backyard beauty

Make it blossom using rectangles. Crop the photos, cut or tear the papers, even choose a metal plaque embellishment—all rectangular. This example combines 24 rectangles in harmonious, stunning radiance.

Place the torn-vellum headline over a row of photo strips.

Liven up the background with layered card stock strips.

Choose a mat color that coordinates with the pictured blooms.

QUICK TIP

Make a simple photo spectacular by cutting it into equal horizontal or vertical strips.

materials

- photos
- 12-inch square of olive green card stock
- card stock in dark raspberry, light raspberry, and light olive
- olive vellum
- small metal floral plaque
- eyelets and eyelet tool
- computer and printer
- adhesive

QUICK TIP

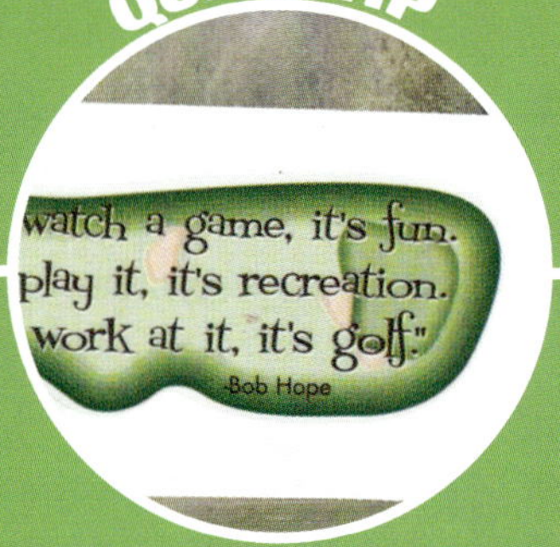

Cover an unimportant part of a photo with a quotation or journaling.

golf

Make it quicker than you can say "Fore!" by combining large photos and stickers on a solid-color card stock background. Choose three photos to tell the story and angle one for pizzazz. Fill in the blank areas with stickers and journaling.

materials

- photos
- 12-inch square of green card stock
- card stock in white and light green
- golf stickers
- eyelets and eyelet tool
- paper trimmer
- adhesive

Angle a photo for flair. Mount the photo on white to contrast with the background.

Place a sticker on card stock, trim, and glue to an open area in the photograph.

fall is in the air

Make it sideways by placing a wide headline strip down the left side to create instant drama. To mimic the look print the headline directly on a sheet of card stock. Readability is enhanced if the headline reads from bottom to top rather than stacking letters on top of each other.

QUICK TIP

Arrange the sticker to lead the eye from the start to finish.

Mat headline block to extend the full length of the page.

Divide the remaining space into two colors to coordinate with the photos.

Mat only one photo to create a focal point.

Align photos on the page, positioning a strip of coordinating card stock to balance if needed.

materials

- photos
- 12-inch square of brown card stock
- card stock in dark green, light green, tan, white, and brown
- leaf sticker
- computer and printer
- date stamp
- swirl punch
- adhesive

autumn

Make it fast with blocks of textured card stock that provide interest and movement. Mount the photos on the same color to simplify the matting. For the background cut two contrasting strips of card stock,

materials

- photos
- 12-inch squares of textured card stock in burnt orange, olive, gold, and red
- blue textured card stock
- autumn die cut
- leaf punches
- black fine-line marking pen
- paper trimmer
- adhesive

Use a computer to print journaling on color card stock.

Choose a die cut with a white background to stand out from the color background.

placing the darker color on the bottom for weight. Sprinkle the paper strips with punched autumn leaves for a layout that you'll fall for throughout all the seasons.

QUICK TIP

Use a purchased die cut to provide a two-second headline.

Use a leaf punch to make colorful die cuts that relate to the theme.

butterfly garden

Make it naturally using several nature shots and a green background. To make a chalklike background even richer, randomly stamp flowers, bees, and dragonflies. To make a column for journaling, cut a 3½-inch-wide strip from peach paper using

materials

- photos
- 12-inch squares of green and peach textured paper
- 12-inch square of peach speckled paper
- rubber stamps in daisy, dragonfly, and bee designs
- ocher ink pad
- white card stock
- paper cutter
- decorative-edge scissors
- transfer lettering and ruled embellishments
- die-cut butterfly
- butterfly stickers
- round paper punch
- scissors
- adhesive

Place butterfly stickers to appear as though in flight or resting on the page.

Stamp subtle designs on the background paper.

Use a die cut to reinforce the theme of the page.

decorative-edge scissors and punch holes as desired. Turn over the remaining (cutaway) piece of paper to reveal the white and use to back the peach paper. For headline draw light pencil rules as guides. The rub-on lettering is applied from the center outward to ensure balance.

QUICK TIP

Face photos toward the center of a spread to better frame the pages.

Use rub-ons for the headline and decorative accents.

Trim a journaling strip using decorative-edge scissors and a paper punch.

Turn the remainder of the paper piece over and use this white piece to back the peach paper.

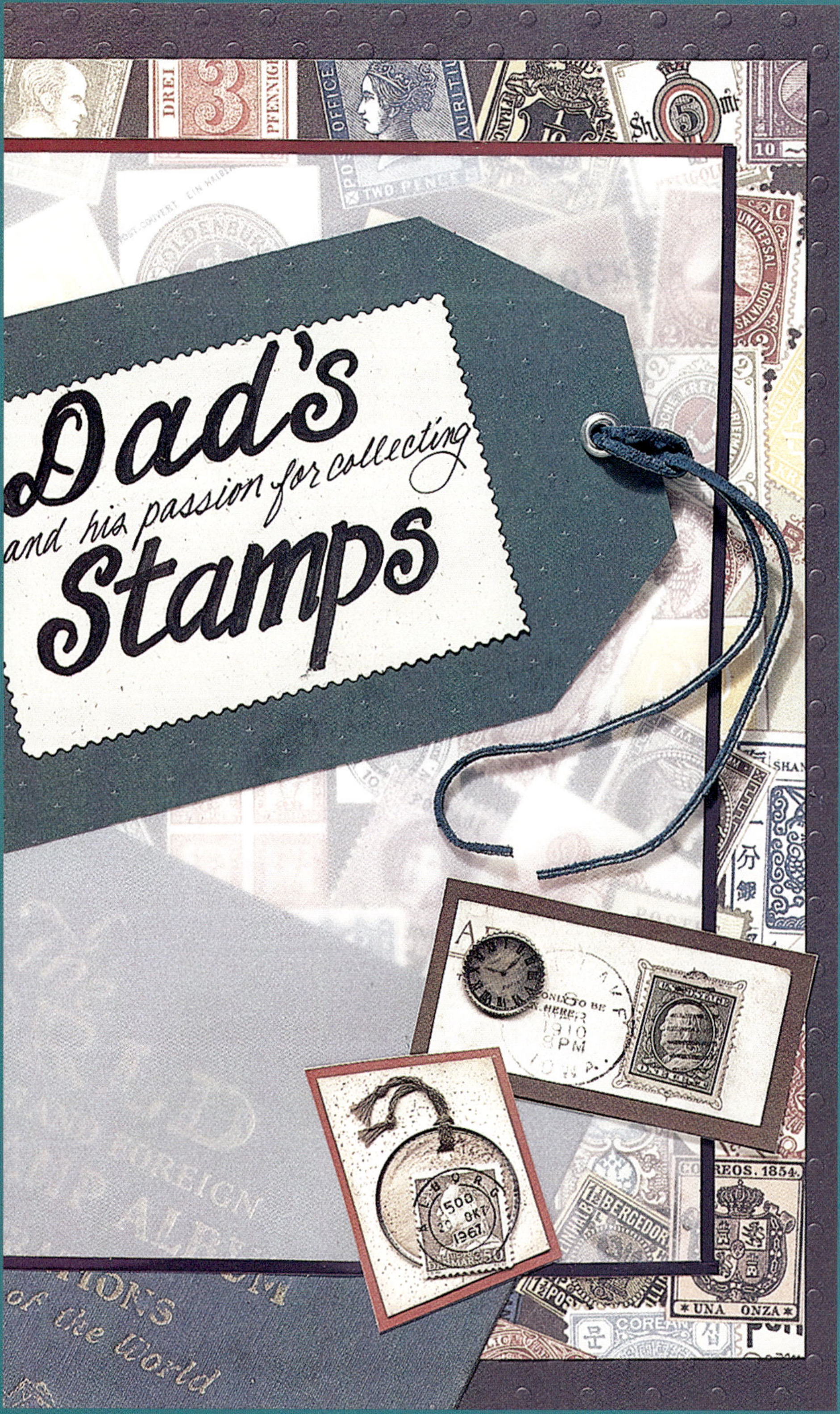
Dad's
and his passion for collecting
Stamps

Enhance vintage photos with easy-to-do accents that are in keeping with the nostalgic theme.

for old time's sake

holy matrimony

Make it authentic using artwork from an 1800s wedding certificate. Make three photocopies of the certificate on *page 347*—one reduced at 67 percent, one enlarged at 140 percent, and one enlarged at 220 percent. On the reduced copy, trim the certificate and personalize

materials

- photo
- two 12-inch squares of parchment paper
- papers in black and rust
- reduced photocopy of vintage marriage certificate, page 347
- enlarged photocopies of marriage certificate for borders and photo mat
- photocopy of black polka-dot papers, felt photo mat, and headline, page 349
- black fine-line and wide permanent marking pens
- scissors
- adhesive

Tip a black rectangular paper to create a shadow.

Fill in the certificate on page 347 with family wedding information.

Outline the pieces in black to create a guide and shadow.

the blanks. Trim the 140-percent enlargement, as shown to use beneath the photo mat. Use the remaining enlargement for the floral strips, headline, and cutouts. The photo mat, polka-dot strips, and outer triangles can be cut from the full-size elements on *page 349.*

Cut out sections of the enlarged copy of the certificate for floral accents.

Cut out this ready-made mat to frame a wedding photo with vintage style.

Cut strips of polka-dot paper to make striking accents.

QUICK TIP

Outline art with a wide black marking pen and crop to leave borders.

Art in back of book!

see pages 347 and 349

QUICK TIP

Chalk the edges to create a shadow.

william and meta

Make it floral using paper and silk bouquets. To make the flowers in the lower right-hand corner, punch out various size flowers from card stock. Immerse the pieces in water and then crumple into balls. Partially uncrumple and let them dry.

materials

- photo
- 12-inch squares of background paper
- patterned paper
- colored card stock
- flower and fern punches
- glue dots
- tweezers
- scissors
- silk flowers
- moiré fabric
- dark green suede paper
- fiber
- bow template
- chalk
- photo corners
- adhesive

Use a template to create a bow for the bouquet.

For dimension adhere the handmade blooms with glue dots.

Use moiré fabric as an appropriate wedding accent.

Make a mini bouquet using tiny silk flowers.

stylish

Make it dressy with the look of clothing. To create a collar, cut a line 5 inches down the center of one paper square and fold as a collar; hold in place using adhesive dots. Punch circle buttons from red suede paper. Chalk the button and lapel edges.

QUICK TIP

Use a white gel pen to make highlights.

Fold back the paper corners to resemble a collar.

Duplicate items in a photo by drawing them on paper and silhouetting them.

Glue the suit jacket to a separate piece of paper.

Mount the photos and journaling on suede paper.

materials

- photo
- two 12-inch squares of background paper
- red suede paper
- chalk
- Pop Dots
- gel pen
- circle punch
- colored paper
- adhesive

growing up

Make it soft and rugged at the same time using cream and brown tones and lace and leather accents. To make the leather-looking vertical bands, cut two 12-inch-long strips of embossed wallpaper border. Use brown shoe polish on a rag to color the strips;

materials

- photos
- two 12-inch squares of neutral card stock
- embossed wallpaper border
- brown shoe polish (liquid or paste)
- clean rag
- black paper
- alphabet stickers in black and gold
- brown textured paper
- black fine-line marking pen
- crocheted lace
- buttons
- wire cutters
- pearls
- thick white crafts glue
- adhesive

Apply shoe polish to a wallpaper border to create a rich texture.

Use snippets of lace, buttons, and pearls for vintage charm.

Layer gold lettering over black to create an instant shadow.

let them dry. The journaling pieces are created by tearing a square and a rectangle from brown textured paper. Add black around the torn edges, allowing it to bleed slightly.

QUICK TIP

Balance a spread using a large photo on one page and several small photos on the other.

Tear textured paper and ink the edge for old-looking paper pieces.

Use crafts glue to hold the dimensional trims in place.

dad's stamps

Make it a collection of the things you love. These incorporate photos of the man who obtained the stamps as well as his children admiring his work, plus bits of the collection itself and theme-related papers. To tone down the postage stamp paper, use

materials

- photos
- 12-inch squares of solid-color background paper
- 12-inch square of postage stamp paper
- 12-inch square of vellum
- photocopy of stamp book cover
- border line stickers
- colored paper scraps
- postage stamp-related cutouts
- decorative-edge scissors with a postage stamp edge pattern
- eyelets in desired colors and shapes, eyelet tool, paper punch
- leather lacing in desired colors
- vellum envelope
- nonvaluable postage stamps
- black marking pen
- adhesive

Apply adhesive strategically so the top cutouts cover the marks.

Apply line stickers in colors that coordinate with the stamp paper to define and secure the vellum edge.

Use vintage-looking cutouts to add interesting shapes and postmarks.

a square of vellum to cover the center portion, allowing the border to remain bright. This same technique is used on the right-hand page as stamps peek from a vellum envelope.

QUICK TIP

Use black and white photos to stand out on a colorful background.

Include nonvaluable stamps to add a personal touch.

Use a wavy decorative-edge scissor to reinforce the stamp theme.

Create paper tags by clipping the corners from one end of a rectangle.

kids of the '60s

Make it speak of a decade using your childhood photos, toys, books, greeting cards, or other items related to an era. Place these items flat in a rectangular arrangement with the most important items around the edges (because photos will cover most of the center area). Photograph your items straight down. To make the final paper appear screened back so that it doesn't appear overly colorful

materials

- photos
- camera
- cherished items, such as a storybook, old watch, harmonica, jump rope, airplane, slingshot, paddleball, jacks, billfold, dolls, or other toys
- photocopier or computer, scanner, and printer
- patterned paper for title
- black and white photos
- brown background paper
- white paper
- gray translucent paper
- decorative-edge scissors
- black marking pen
- adhesive

Photograph arranged items for a unique background.

Use gray translucent papers to create shadows.

Choose an appropriate paper on which to print a computer-generated title.

and overpowering, do a creative enlargement either on your computer or on a photocopier. If you have a computer, you may be able to scan and lighten the image. Or use a photocopier and light control to alter the colors.

QUICK TIP

Choose items with the same color scheme to be photographed for a cohesive background.

Handwrite journaling with a black marking pen.

Use decorative-edge scissors to trim white squares.

QUICK TIP

Use a toothpick to apply tiny dots of glue to an accent.

grandpa's music

Make it harmonious by highlighting a music-related photo with papers, charms, and a paper cutout that carry the theme. To remove the charm rings, carefully bend back and forth using a needle-nose pliers. Glue in place using a small amount of clear adhesive.

materials

- photo
- 8½×11-inch piece of neutral music-note paper
- 12-inch square of vintage-looking neutral background paper
- music-staff charms
- needle-nose pliers
- black photo corners
- glue stick
- large black music-staff die-cut
- toothpick
- medium-tip metallic gold marking pen
- gold press-on lettering
- black fine-tip marking pen
- clear adhesive for metal
- adhesive

Glue metal charms to the page for sparkle and dimension.

Use a die cut to reinforce the theme of the page.

Draw rules to guide handwriting.

Draw a light rule around the page for a vintage look.

beekeeper

Make it as sweet as honey by layering textures. Adhere a sheer layer of paper to the page. Place a panel of netting along the left side. Apply spray adhesive to that area only. Place a layer of gold tissue over the netting, press down firmly, and trim the edges even.

QUICK TIP

Seal clover between clear acid-free plastic to protect the page if desired.

materials

- photos
- 12-inch square of background paper
- sheer paper
- gold tissue paper
- card stock in green and ivory
- netting
- paper cutter
- corner punch
- crafts knife
- embossing template and stylus
- dried pressed clover or flowers
- black marking pen
- glue dots
- gold gel pen
- spray adhesive
- adhesive

Use netting to resemble beehive texture.

Cut a perfect oval using a template.

Use a corner rounder on the mat.

Add texture by layering gold tissue over fabric.

QUICK TIP

Use feather stickers if real feathers are not available or desired.

big horse

Make it a story with a photograph accompanied by a newspaper article. Start with a print of your photograph. A photocopy will not work because the ink will run when painted. To tint areas use very little watercolor paint thinned with water. Let the paint dry.

materials

- photo
- 8½×11-inch piece of tan or ivory paper
- 12-inch square of red background paper
- coordinating paper, such as natural brown
- crafts knife or paper cutter
- ruler
- watercolor paints
- small watercolor paintbrush
- computer and printer
- newspaperlike font
- feathers
- alphabet paper
- adhesive

Tear paper edges to add soft lines to the page.

Print on tan paper to give the text an aged appearance.

Embellish with elements that help to tell the story.

john and dorothy

Make it quicker than you can say "I do!" using the floral art from *page 351*. ut the cream-color paper approximately ¼ inch smaller than the ocher background. Copy two sets of the photo corners, one at 100 percent and one at 50 percent.

Affix the trimmed floral frame over the solid color, then trim edges with crafts knife and straightedge.

Choose solid colors to coordinate with your photo.

Use colored marker to coordinate with the artwork.

Choose from three sets of floral art on page 351.

QUICK TIP

Make several photocopies of artwork to have on hand for other pages.

materials

- photo
- papers or photocopied papers, page 351
- cream and ochre-color papers
- computer scanner and printer or photocopier
- paper cutter
- crafts knife
- scissors
- straightedge
- adhesive

see page 351

QUICK TIP

Use paper edges to align rub-on lettering.

grandmother

Make it bejeweled with gems and fancy buttons. To color details of the photo, use dull-pointed colored pencils. To transfer lettering, draw a guide using a vanishing-ink pen. Use a dull pencil to rub over the letters to transfer them. Add emphasis to the first letter with gems.

materials

- black and white photo in vintage mat
- 12-inch square of parchment paper
- rub-on or sticker lettering in large and small sizes
- vanishing ink pen
- buttons
- press-on gems
- thick white crafts glue
- colored pencils
- hat box, advertising, magazine, store bag, or other item relating to the time period, to be photocopied
- adhesive

Apply press-on vintage font lettering for journaling.

Photocopy a vintage hatbox or other advertising piece to use as a banner in the background.

Use press-on gems and pearls to add sparkle to the design.

Decorate the photo mat with vintage buttons.

skating in 1969

Make it frosty with dotted vellum, snowflake sequins, and seed beads. Type text on a computer and print it on vellum. Adhere the photo to vellum. Position the vellum over the papers and tack in place by sewing snowflakes and beads over background. Knot on the back.

Adhere red paper vertically to the white mat.

Space dots between numbers to make the date the same length as the title.

Overlay dotted vellum for the appearance of snow.

Sew snowflake sequins on paper and hold in place with tiny seed beads.

QUICK TIP

To make solid vellum appear dotted, use a wide white marker to make flecks.

materials

- photo
- $8\frac{1}{2}\times11$-inch pieces of black, blue, red, and dotted vellum
- two $8\frac{1}{2}\times11$-inch pieces of white paper
- computer and printer
- paper cutter
- snowflake sequins in red and white
- clear seed beads
- beading needle
- white thread
- adhesive

our first home

Make it full with in-depth journaling, several photos, and a headline that spans both pages. Alphabet stickers make this process quick and easy. To balance the pages place vertical paper bands along the outer edges. Depending on the size and shape of your photos, leave

materials

- photos
- 12-inch squares of patterned background paper
- patterned paper for journaling
- dark green card stock
- fern stamp
- ink pads in two shades of green
- paper cutter
- alphabet stickers
- key die cuts
- adhesive

Place vertical paper panels on the outer edge of each page to create balance.

Randomly stamp green card stock with a fern stamp and cut to make photo mats.

Use purchased die-cut accents to reinforce the house theme.

QUICK TIP

Group letter stickers to make words appear as a block.

space around each one or overlap some slightly, being cautious of what is covered. Divide the journaling into blocks to keep the pages organized and easy to read. Handwrite, type, or print the journaling using a vintage-looking font.

Use ornate alphabet stickers to make a fancy headline.

Choose a subtle-print background paper for journal blocks.

grandma's cookies

Make it a recipe for success using vintage kitchen towel motifs to accent recipe pages. If your towel includes characters, photocopy them using a mirror-image setting to allow them to face the characters opposite. If you don't have a vintage towel, check

materials

- photo
- 12-inch squares of white background paper
- vintage kitchen towel
- five patterned background papers to coordinate with towel
- 8½×11-inch piece of white paper
- 8½×11-inch piece of parchment paper
- wooden fork and spoon (toy size or full-size kitchen utensils)
- white crafting foam
- recipes on cards
- silver alphabet stickers
- scissors
- adhesive

Place a single photo prominently under the heading.

Separate the photo from the towel-print background with colorful mats.

Photocopy a vintage kitchen towel to make a unique paper background.

antiques stores and flea markets for a towel or vintage fabric. Photocopy a toy wooden spoon and fork. Silhouette the pieces and mount them to strips of foam to make them stand out on the page. If using full-size wooden utensils, reduce the size to fit the page.

QUICK TIP

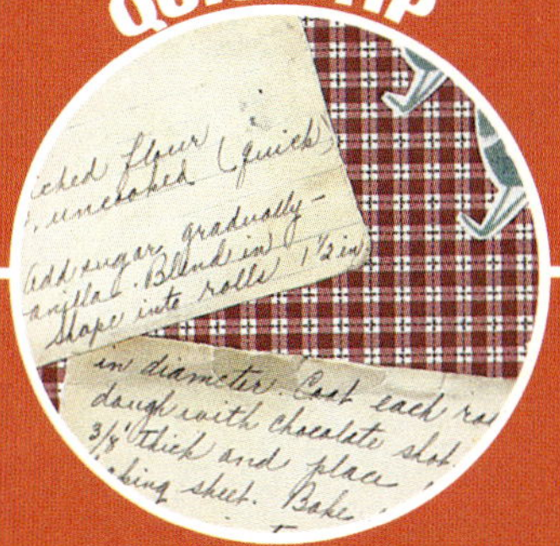

Photocopy recipe cards in color to reveal the well-used patina.

Place strips of three background papers horizontally to add continuity to the spread.

Photocopy images using a mirror-image setting so the characters face across the spread.

Mount photocopied utensils on crafting foam strips to make them pop from the page.

Silhouetted towel motifs march on various horizon lines.

richard and sally

Make it antiqued by accenting photos with cream paper doilies and photocopies of family heirlooms. Look at each doily center to determine how much edge you would like showing. Experiment with a variety of crop sizes on scrap paper before cutting a photograph.

materials

- photos
- 12-inch squares of patterned background paper
- antique-style decorative-edge scissors
- 8-inch square and 4-inch round ivory paper doilies
- photocopies of vintage items
- ivory parchment paper
- lace-style border stickers
- disappearing-ink pen
- ruler
- black fine-line marking pen
- adhesive

Use a ruler and a disappearing-ink pen to mark straight rules for journaling.

Make the initial letter larger than the journaling.

Photocopy metal and glass items to highlight the design.

Crop photos using decorative-edge scissors to fit on a doily. Size by cutting paper scraps to fit the doily.

To adhere the doilies to background paper and to prevent damaging the delicate paper, spray each back with a light coat of adhesive. To add interest and color to the pages, include photocopies of small family heirlooms. Silhouette the items and place around the photos.

QUICK TIP

Use a pin to remove any cutout areas of the doilies that remain intact.

To cut a small silhouette, move the paper rather than the scissors for a nice clean edge.

A lace sticker border softens the hard edge of the parchment paper.

A fleck of ivory in the background paper coordinates well with the ivory lace accents.

glossary

Acid-free

Acid is used in paper manufacturing to break apart the wood fibers and the lignin that holds them together. If acid remains in the materials used for photo albums, it can react chemically with photographs and cause their deterioration. Acid-free products have a pH factor of 7.0 or above. It is imperative that all materials (glue, pens, papers, etc.) used in memory albums or scrapbooks be acid-free.

Acid migration

Acid migration is the transfer of acidity from one item to another through physical contact or acidic vapors. If a newspaper clipping is put into an album, the area it touches will eventually turn yellow or brown. A deacidification pH factor spray can be used on acidic papers, or they can be photocopied onto acid-free papers.

Adhesive

Scrapbooking adhesives include glue sticks, double-sided tape, spray adhesive, thick white crafts glue, mounting tabs, and other products. Read the labels to determine the best adhesive for the intended use.

Archival quality

Archival quality is a term used to indicate materials that have undergone laboratory analysis to determine that their acidic and buffered contents are within safe levels.

Borders

Borders are precut strips of patterned or solid-color paper used to accent a scrapbook page.

Brads

Brads are small metal embellishments that are secured to paper by poking their prongs through the paper and bending the prongs outward from one another.

Buffered paper

During manufacture, a buffering agent, such as calcium carbonate or magnesium bicarbonate, can be added to paper to neutralize acid contaminant. Such papers have a pH of 8.5.

Card stock

Often used for the base or background of a page, card stock is a heavy paper with a smooth surface.

Corner rounder

Used like a paper punch, this tool rounds the corners of a photograph or paper.

Crafts knife

This tool has a small replaceable blade for cutting paper and other materials.

Cropping

Cropping means cutting or trimming a photo to keep only the most important parts of the image.

Decorative-edge scissors

Available in a wide assortment of cutting blades, these scissors cut wavy, scalloped, zigzagged, or other decorative edges in paper and other thin materials.

Die-cut

This is a paper embellishment in which the background has been cut away. Die-cuts come in hundreds of shapes and sizes.

Eyelets

Eyelets are small metal embellishments that have an open circular center. When set, eyelets can attach thin items (such as paper or fabric) or provide a hole for lacing.

Glossy

A smooth, shiny appearance or finish is referred to as glossy.

Glue stick

A glue stick is a solid stick-type glue that is applied by rubbing.

glossary continued

Journaling

Journaling refers to text that provides details about the photographs on a scrapbook page. Journaling can be done in your own handwriting, on a computer, or with adhesive letters, rub-ons, or stencils.

Lignin

Lignin is the material that holds wood fibers together as a tree grows. If lignin remains in the final paper (as with newsprint), it becomes yellow and brittle over time. Most papers other than newsprint are lignin free.

Mat

Mats are varying weights of paper for framing photographs using single or multiple layers.

Matte

A dull surface or finish, not shiny or glossy, is considered matte.

Opaque

Colors that are dense and cannot be seen through are opaque.

Paper punch

This handheld tool punches out circles, hearts, diamonds, and other shapes in stencil form.

Paper trimmer

This paper-cutting tool has a surface for holding the paper and a sharp blade that cuts the paper in a straight line.

pH factor

The pH factor refers to the acidity of a paper. The pH scale, a standard for measurement of acidity and alkalinity, runs from 0 to 14, each number representing a tenfold increase; neutral is 7. Acid-free products have a pH factor of 7 or above. Special pH-tester pens are available to determine the acidity or alkalinity of products.

Photo-safe

Photo-safe is a term similar to archival quality but more specific to materials used with photographs. Acid-free is the determining factor for a product to be labeled photo-safe.

Protective sleeves

Made of plastic to slip over a finished album page, sleeves can be side-loading or top-loading and fit 8½×11-inch or 12-inch-square pages. Choose only acid-free sleeves. Polypropylene (vinyl), commonly available for office use, is not archival quality.

Rubber stamping

Designs are etched into a rubber mat that is applied to a wood block. This rubber design is stamped onto an ink pad to transfer the design to paper or other surfaces.

Scrapbooking papers

Scrapbooking papers are usually 12-inch squares or 8½×11-inch rectangles. These include solids, patterns, textures, and vellum.

Stencil

Made from heavy paper or plastic, a stencil is laid flat on a surface. Paint or other medium is applied through the openings of the design to transfer it.

Stickers

Available in plastic, paper, vinyl, fabric, and other materials, stickers can be peeled from a backing paper and pressed into place.

Tracing paper

A sheer sheet of paper that can be seen through, it is usually used to trace a pattern.

Vellum

Available in white, colors, and patterns, this translucent paper has a frosted appearance.

index

A–B

C

F–G

H

J

K

The following pages provide dozens of patterns and ready-to-go headlines for instant scrapbooking fun!

patterns and headlines

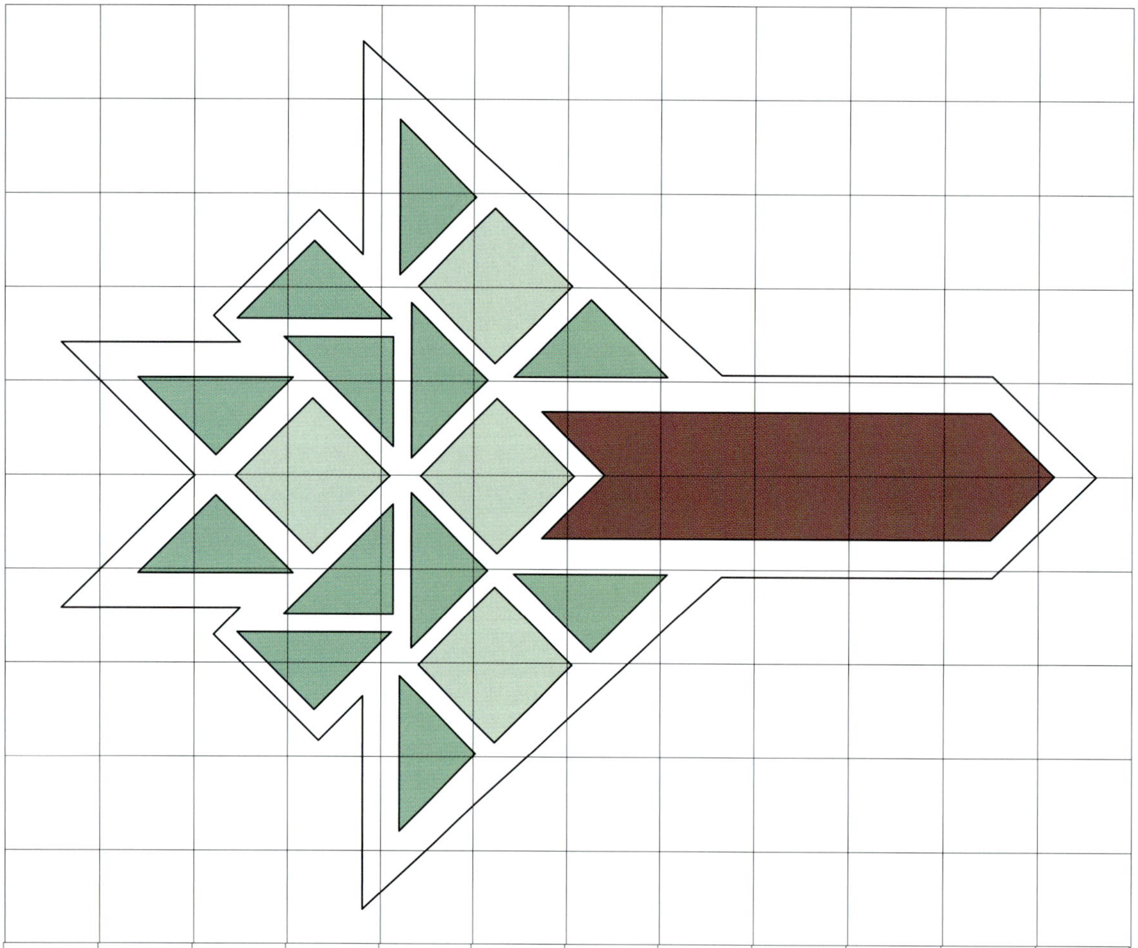

1 SQUARE = 1 INCH

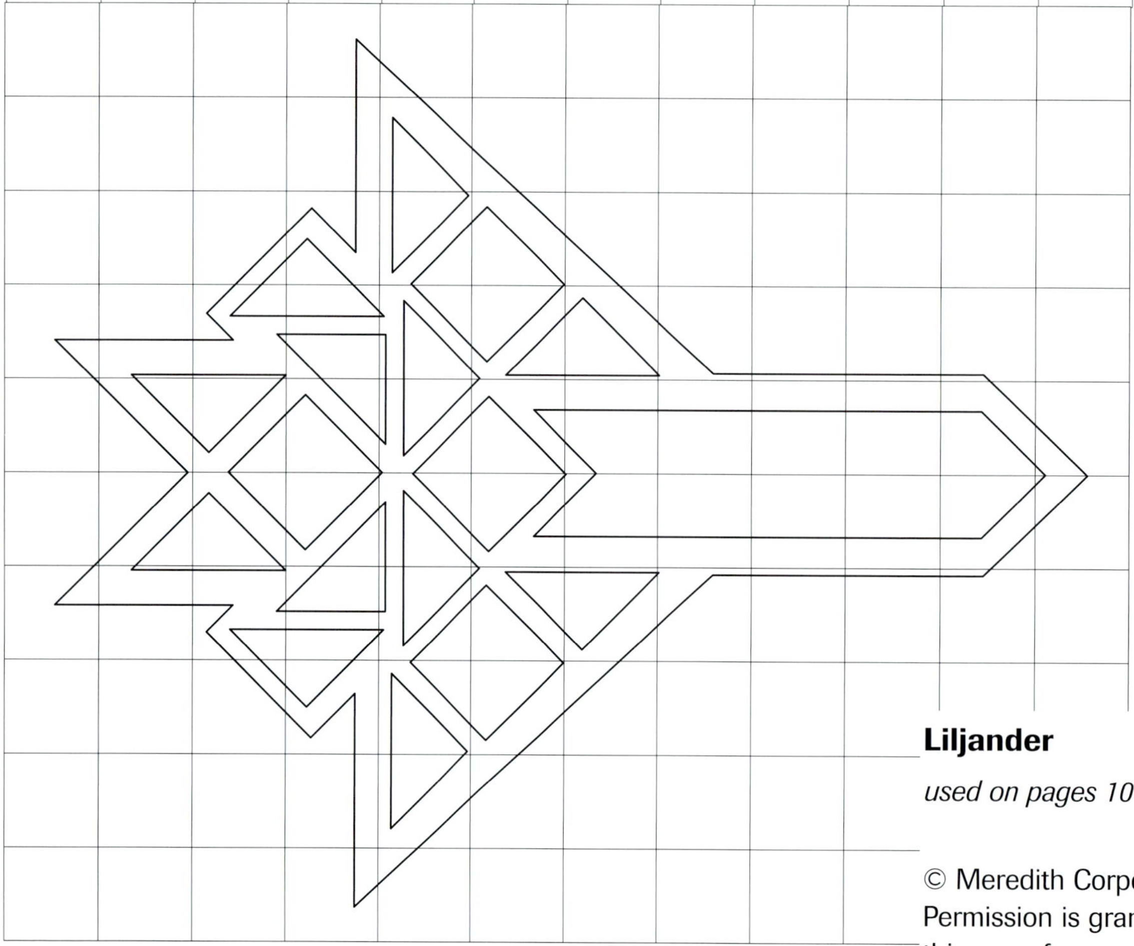

Liljander

used on pages 104–105

FLAG PATTERN

1 SQUARE = 1 INCH

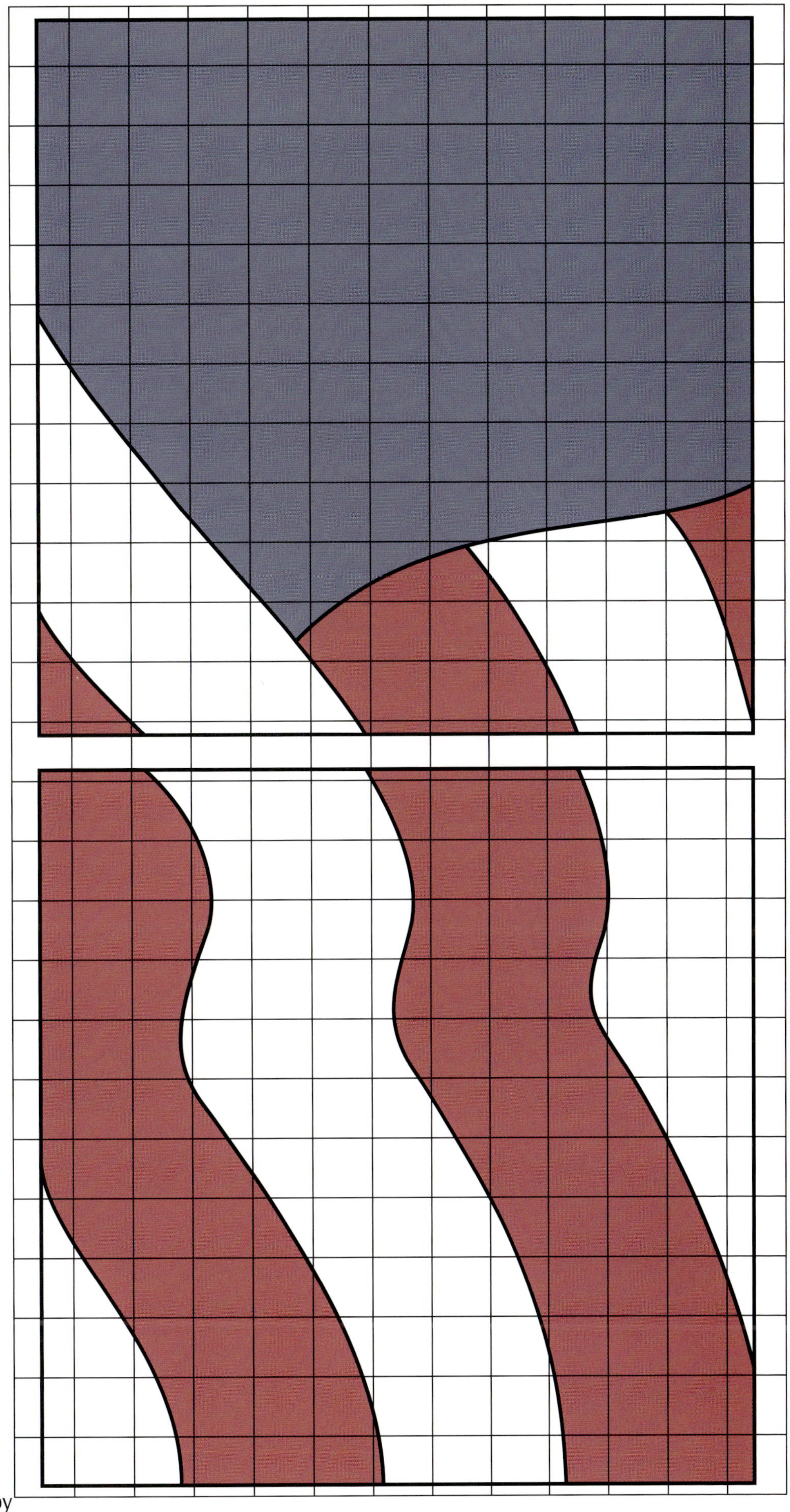

Honorable Duty

used on pages 94–95

1 SQUARE = 1 INCH

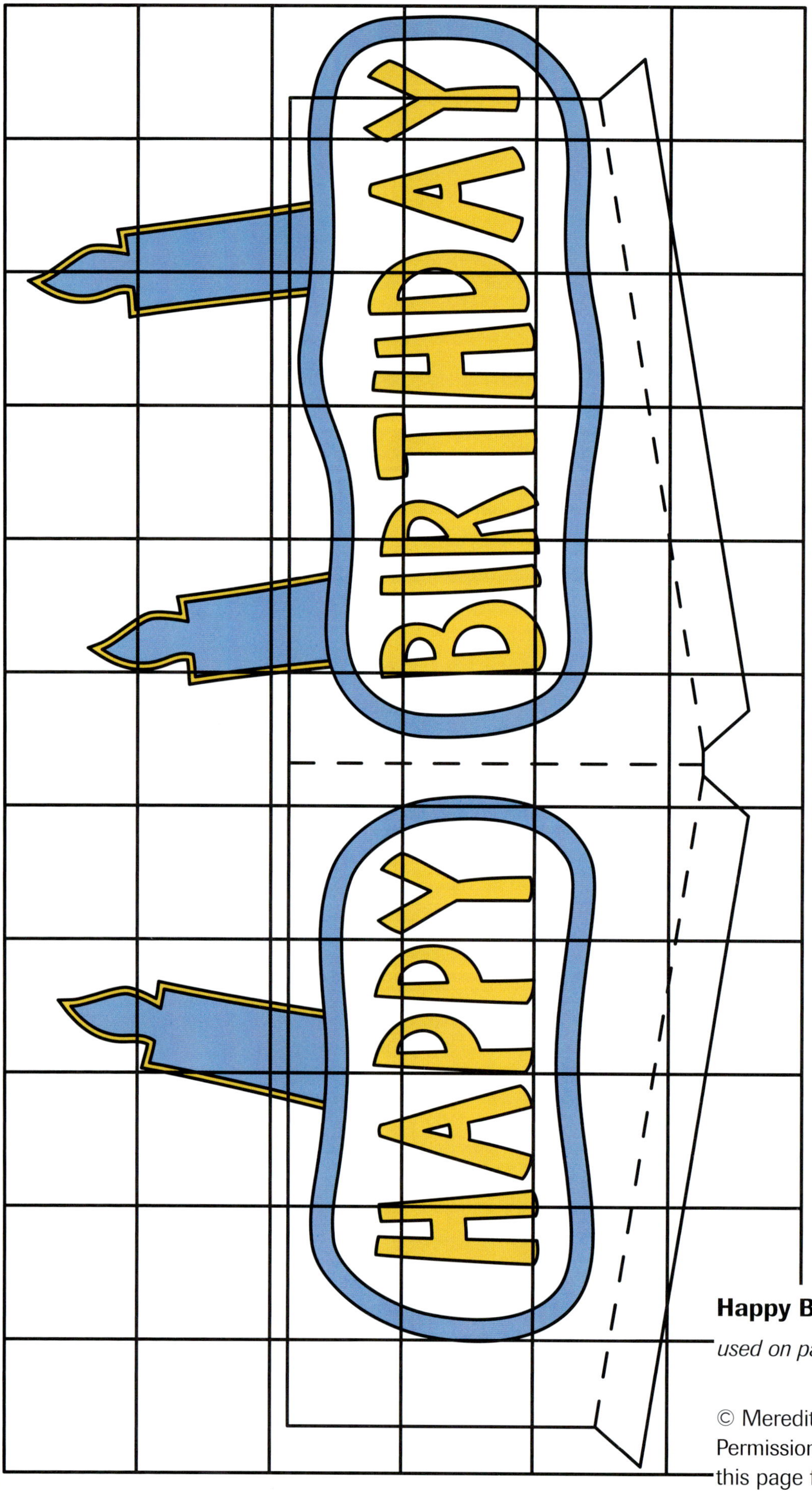

Happy Birthday

used on pages 148–149

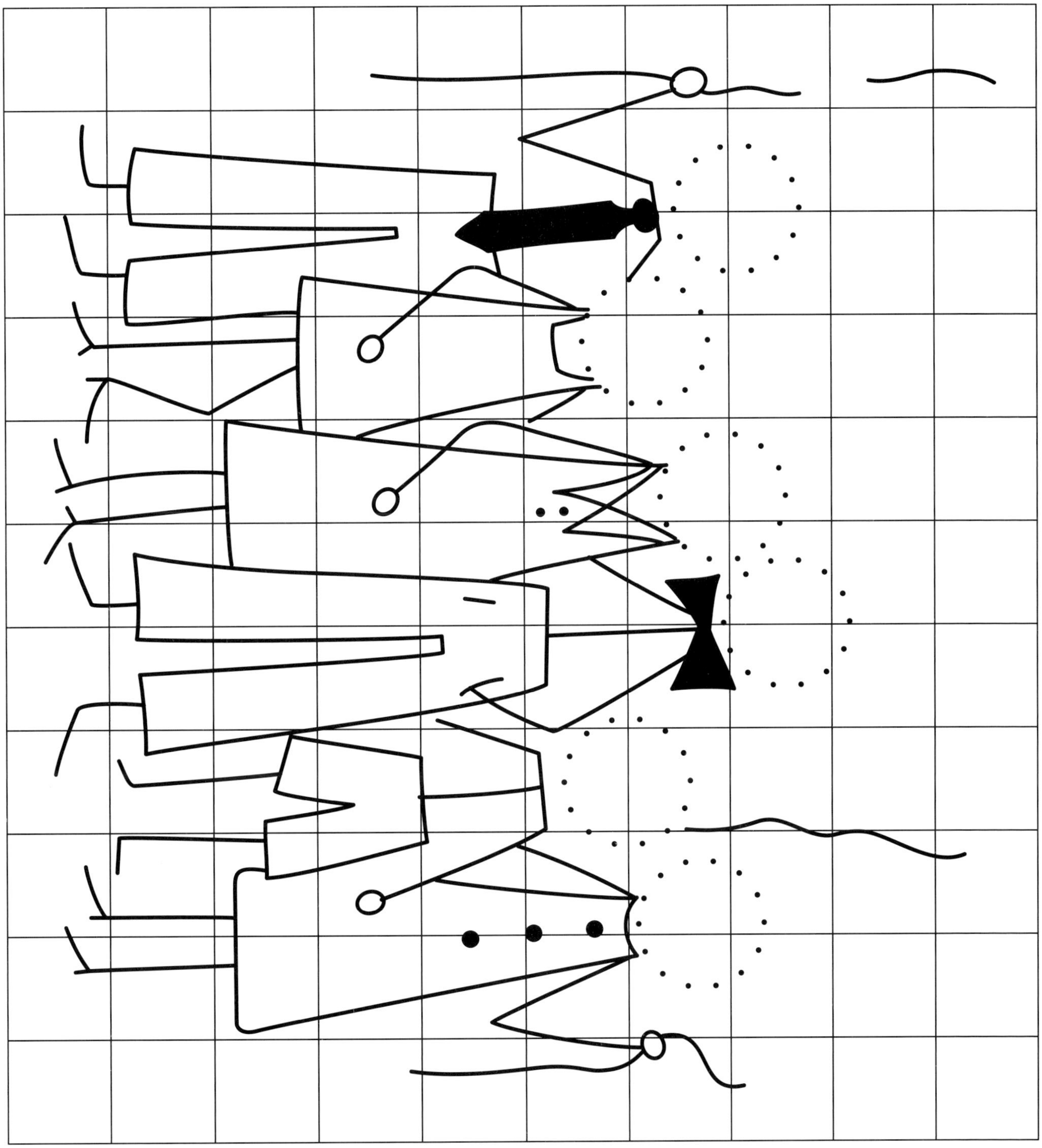

Celebration

used on page 137

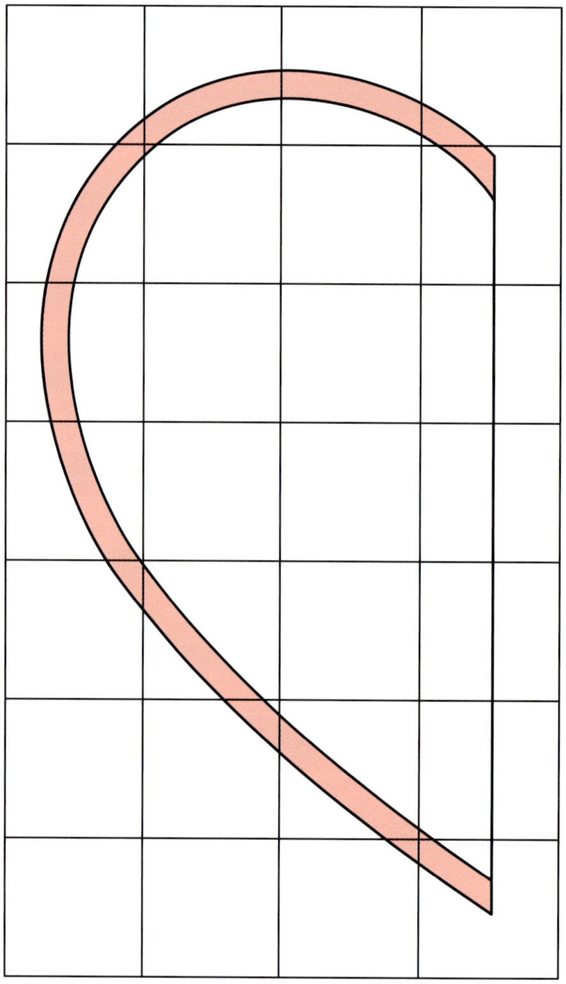

HEART MAT PATTERN 1 SQUARE = 1 INCH

Penny and Frieda

used on pages 116–117

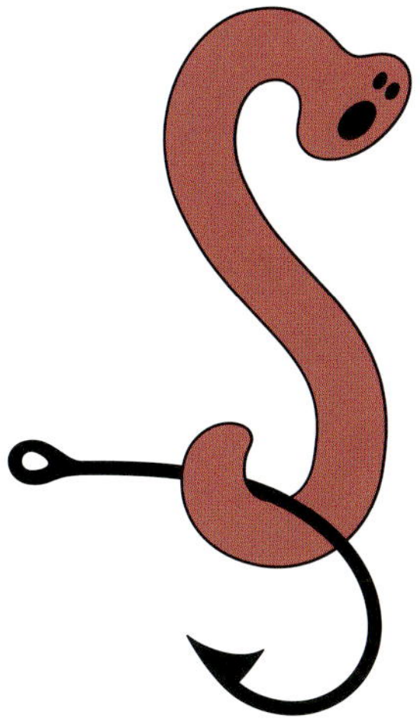

HOOK AND WORM
PATTERN

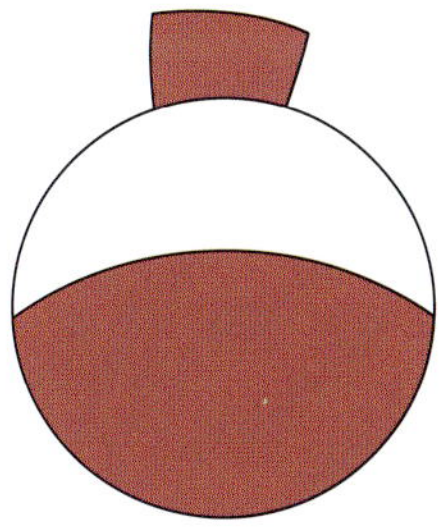

BOBBER PATTERN

Fishing Kids

used on pages 110–111

Use these patterns for the button border on page 79.

Use these patterns to make a border as shown on page 123. To fit a 12-inch page, splice two strips together.

Use this pattern to create a sun headline box as shown on page 188. Color in a strip for the water or use scrapbook paper.

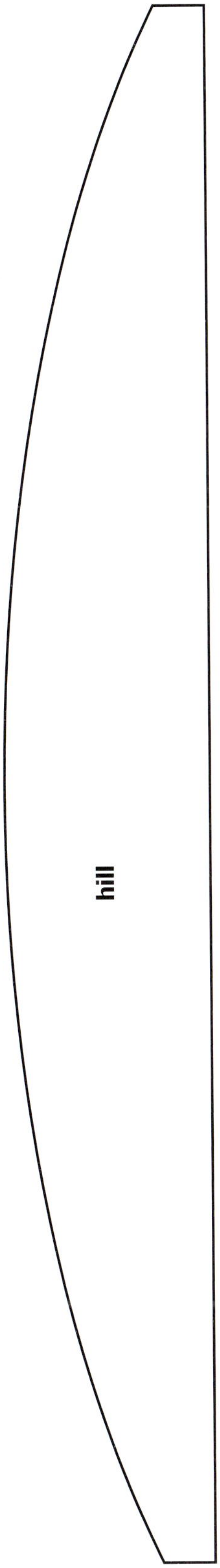

Use these patterns to make a car border as shown on page 187. Make the wheels using two sizes of round paper punches. Detail using a black fine-line marking pen.

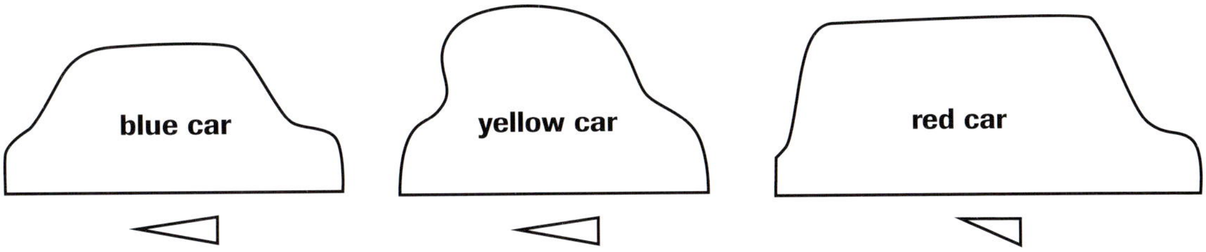

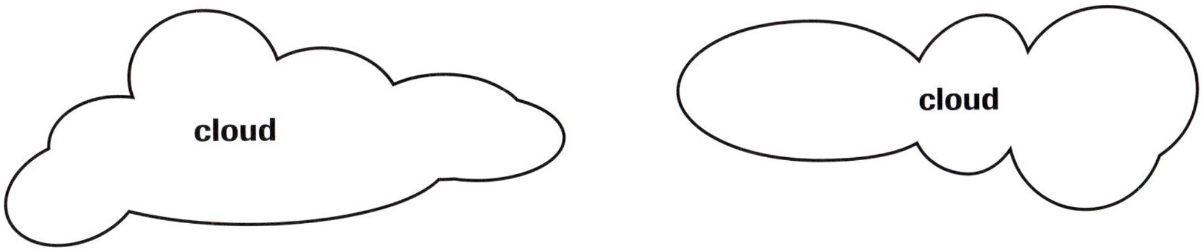

tag patterns

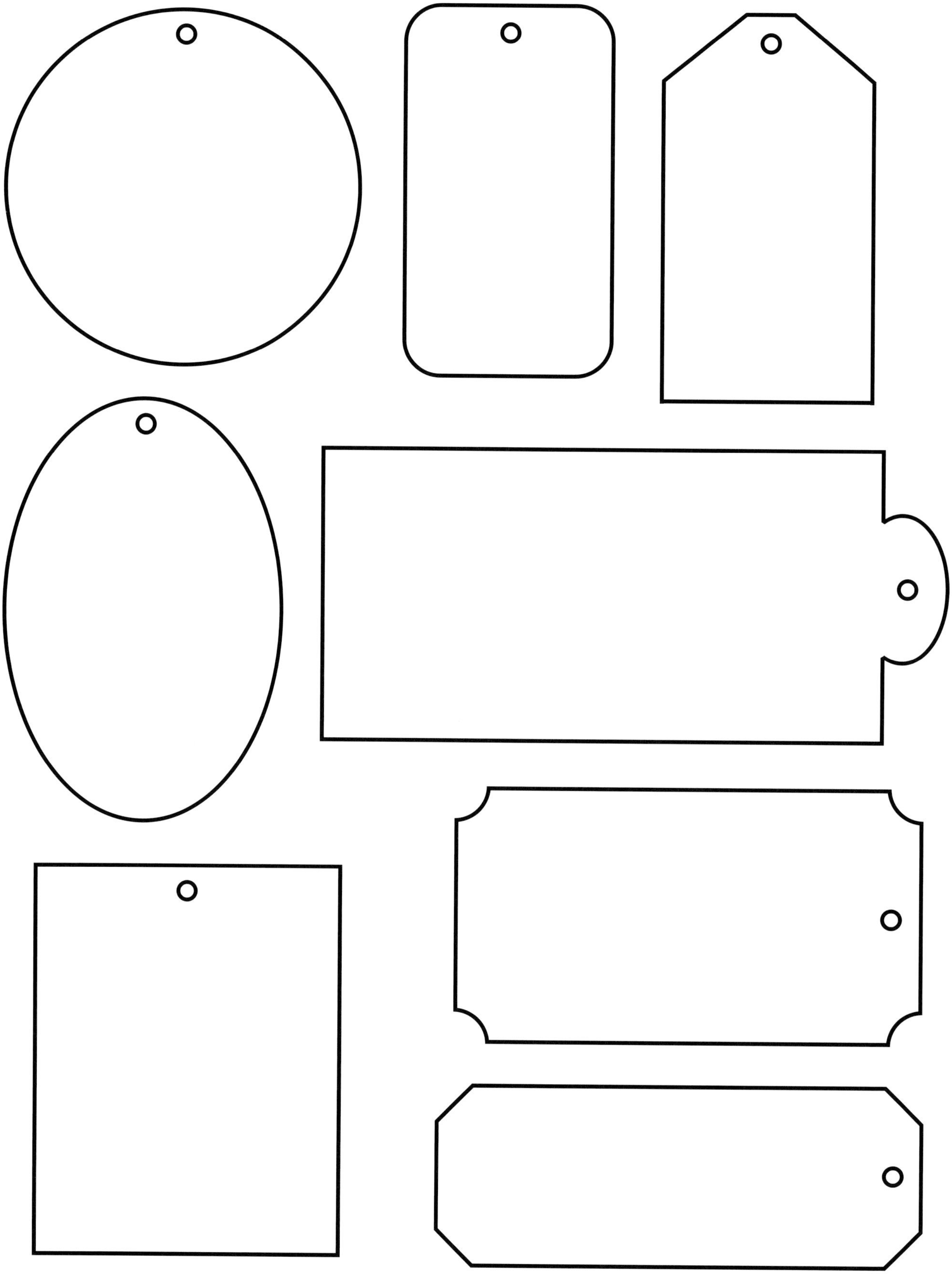

Cute as a Bug!

sweet baby girl

sweet baby boy

OH BABY!

rock-a-bye baby

Sweet thing!

Kids Do the Cutest Things!

girly girl

ALL BOY

Are you cute or what?

Children Are a Blessing

Having Fun with the kids

FAMILY FUN

Having a ball!

Our Goofy Gang

Our Kitty

Our Puppy

Is this fun or what?!

I won't tell if you won't...I won't tell if you won't...I won't tell if you won't...I won't tell if you won't...I won't tell if you won't...

FAMILY IS THE FABRIC OF LIFE

Sisterly Love

brotherly love

Good Ol' Mom

Good Ol' Dad

Let the Games Begin!

LET THE FUN BEGIN

Our Vacation at Last!

A Trip to Remember

Are we there yet?

Ready...Set...Let's Go!

VACATIONS ROCK

stop and smell the flowers

play
BALL!

The Good
Ol' Days

FUN
in the
SUN

Girls just wanna have fun!

Boys just wanna have fun!

family

friends

GROOVY!

Life is good!

Several projects in this book use clever papers, frames, and embellishments—all available on *pages 289–351* for you to photocopy and use in your scrapbooks.

art papers and more

First HAIRCUT

First Tooth

First Step

First Tooth and First Step

used on pages 32–33

Cut out strips along the centers of black lines to make frames.

First Tooth and First Step

used on pages 32–33

Anné Mae

used on page 35

PICTURE MAT

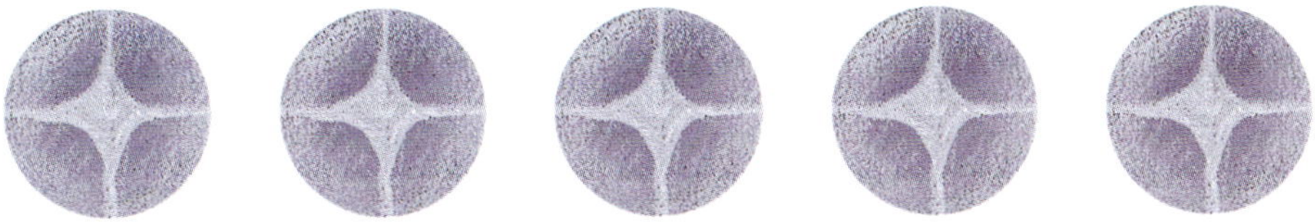

ALTERNATE PHOTO MAT CORNERS

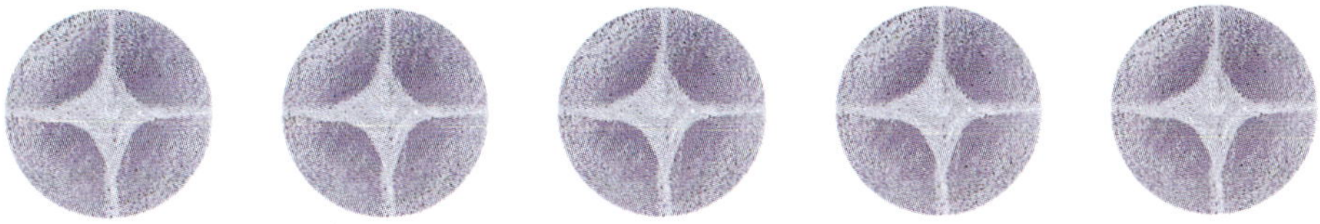

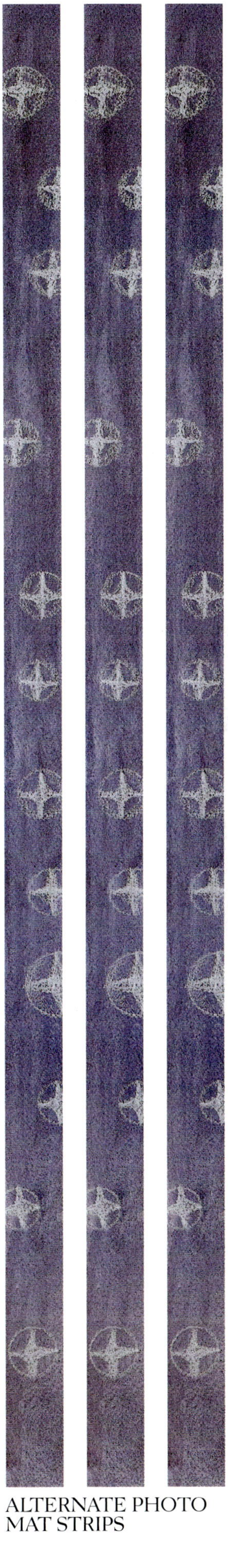

ALTERNATE PHOTO
MAT STRIPS

Anné Mae

used on pages 35

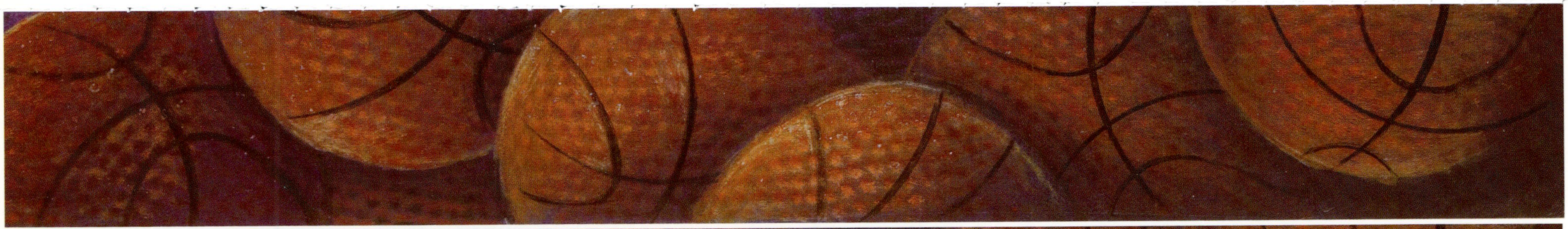

Use the basketball borders to frame photos or the page. To make them 12 inches in length, photocopy them at 115 percent.

Use markers to color in the letters and numbers to suit your needs.

Sep Rams and Two Home Runs

used on pages 47–49

Trim baseball around the outline. Write in your own all-star's signature.

Color in your own scoreboard headline using a bright-color marker for words and a black marker to fill in the rest, as shown on page 48.

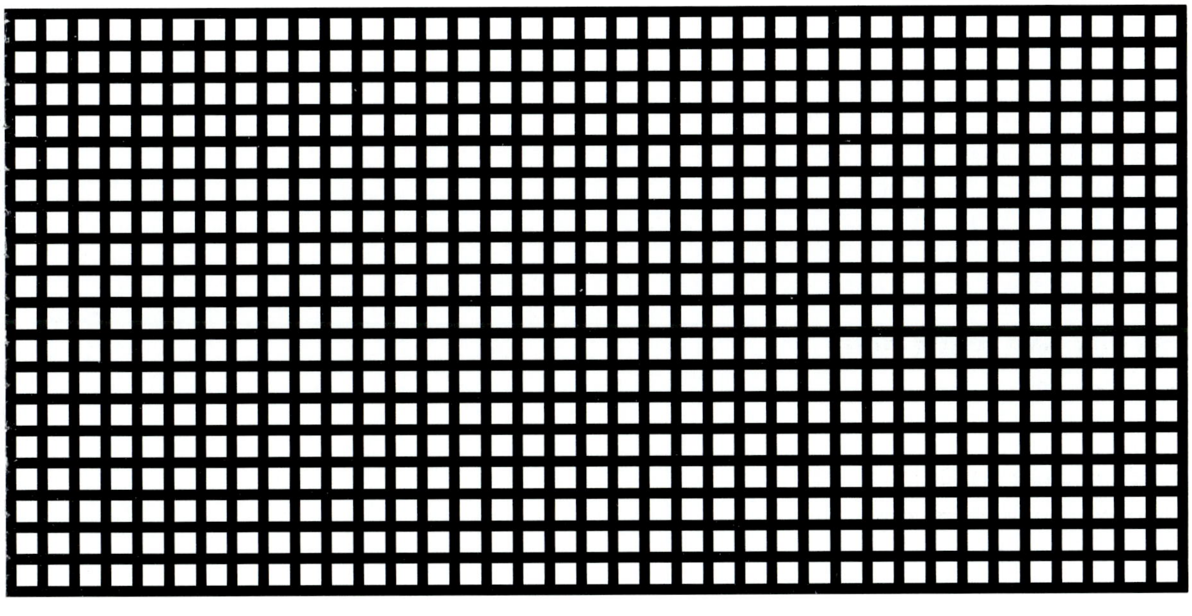

Color stripes with markers in your team colors.

Sep Rams and Two Home Runs

used on pages 47–49

Peas in a Pod

used on page 76

Peas in a Pod

used on page 76

FULL-SIZE JOURNAL BOX

ALTERNATE JOURNAL BOX

ALTERNATE JOURNAL BOX

FULL-SIZE ACCENTS

VINE BORDERS
Enlarge 111 percent for a 12-inch-square page.

Peas in a Pod

used on page 76

FULL-SIZE
PEA POD

ALTERNATE
PEA POD

FULL-SIZE ACCENTS

Peas in a Pod

used on page 76

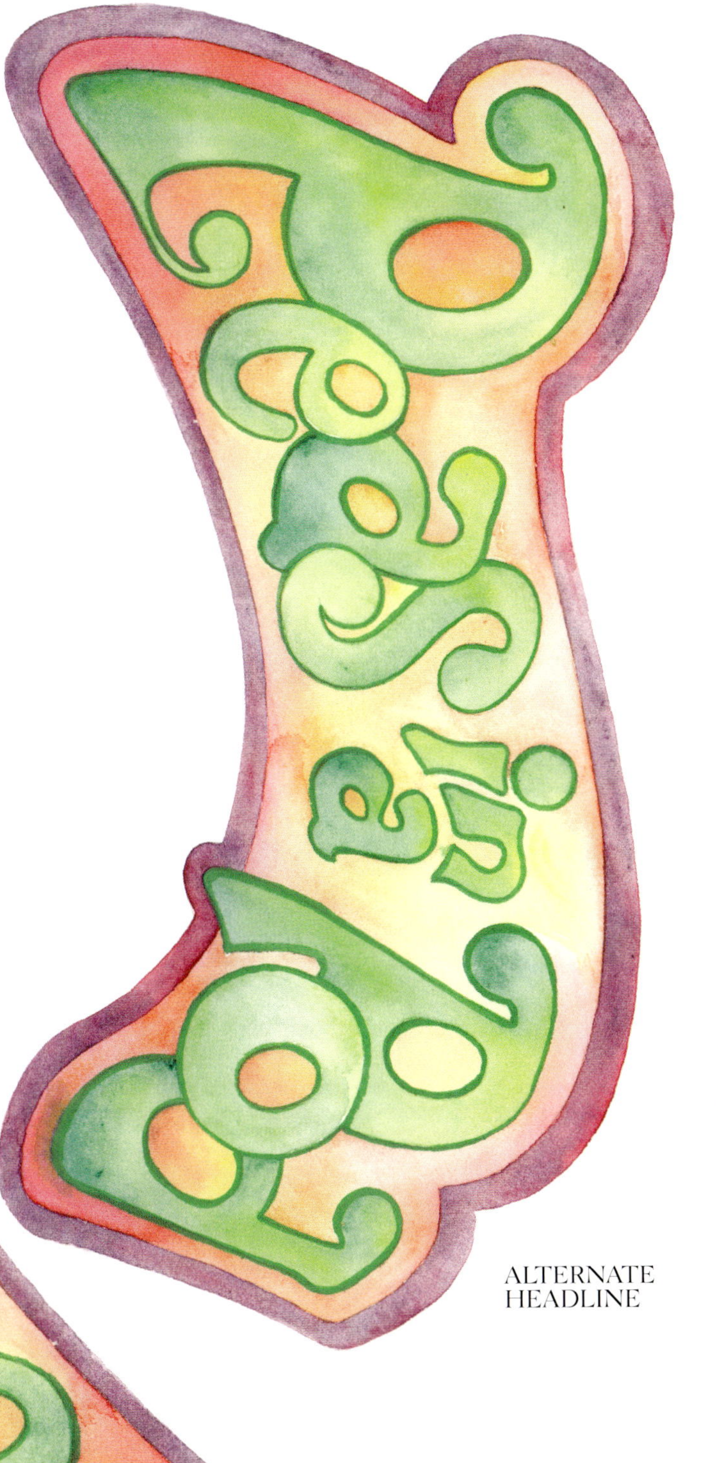

ALTERNATE
HEADLINE

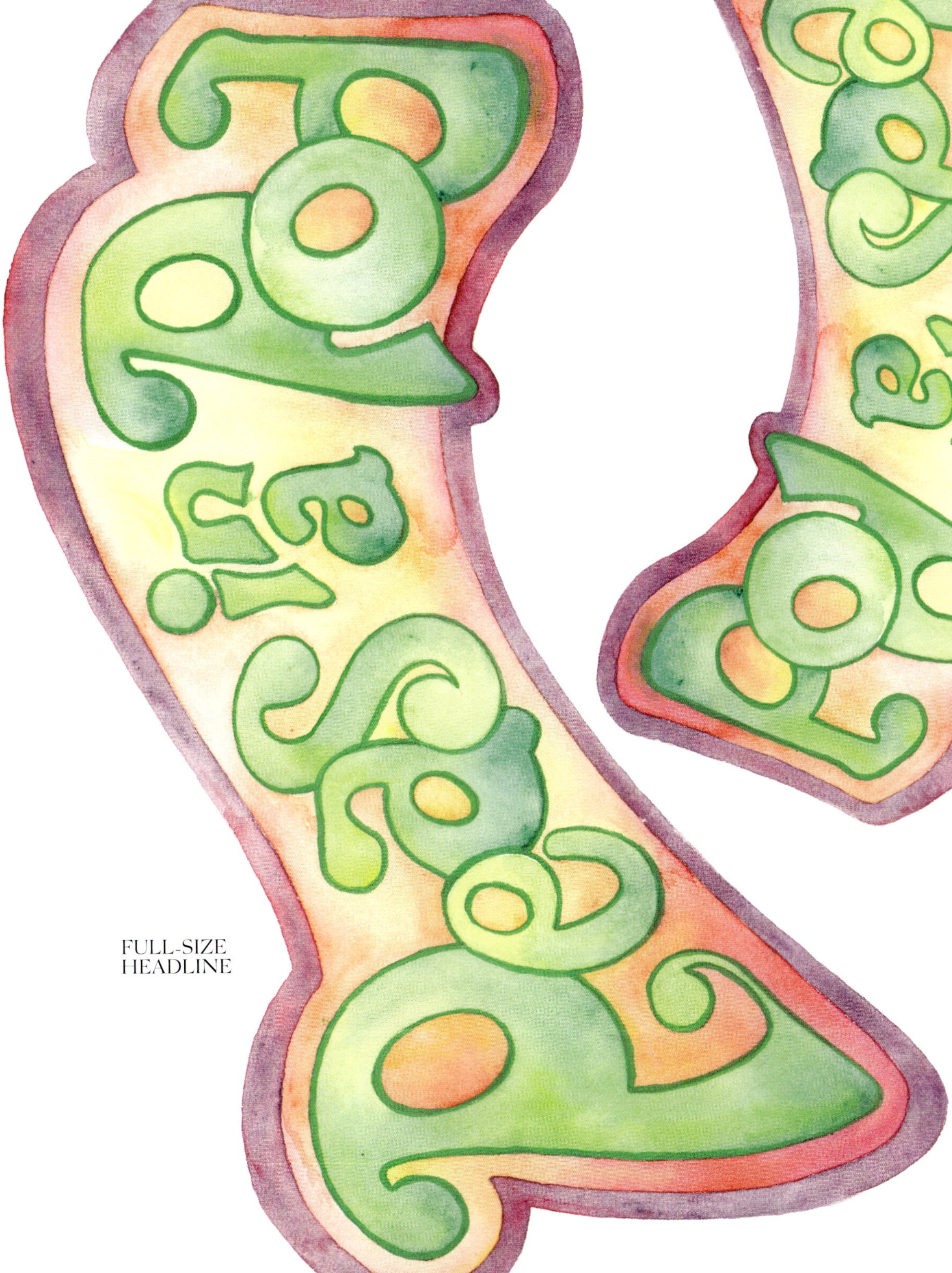

FULL-SIZE
HEADLINE

Peas in a Pod

used on page 76

Cut around individual border designs. Overlap the strips to create frames.

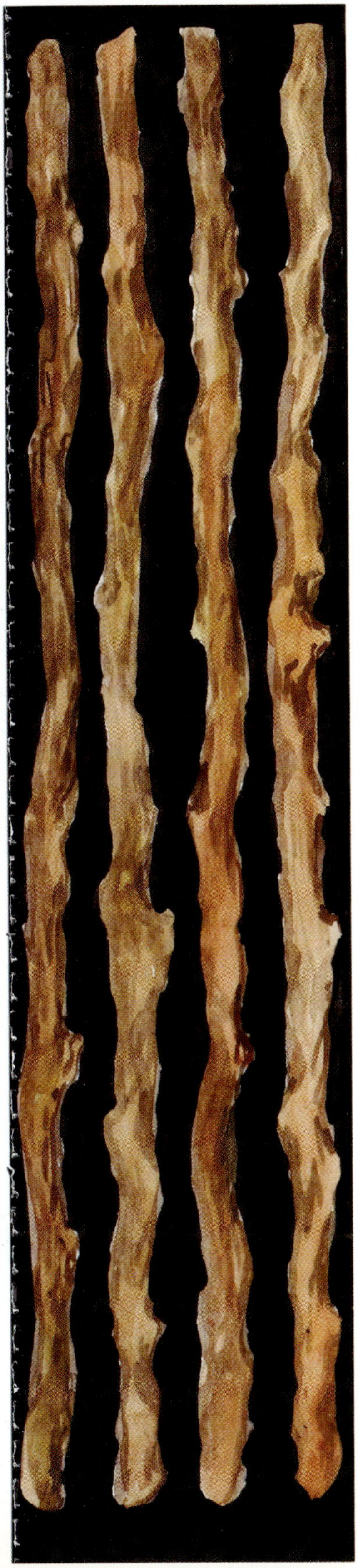

Grampa's Lake

used on page 89

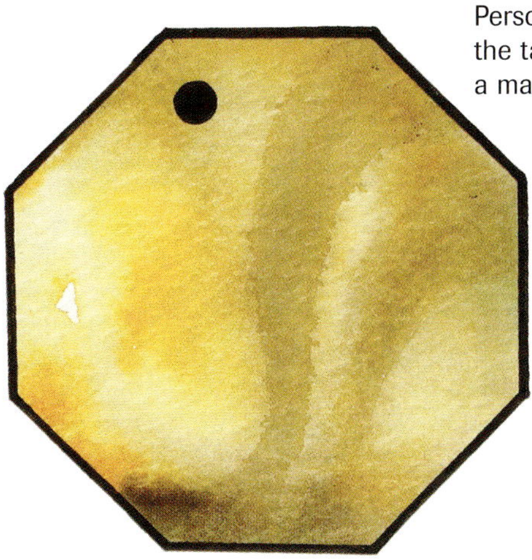

Personalize
the tag with
a marking pen.

Emma and Honey

used on page 129

My Cat

used on page 120

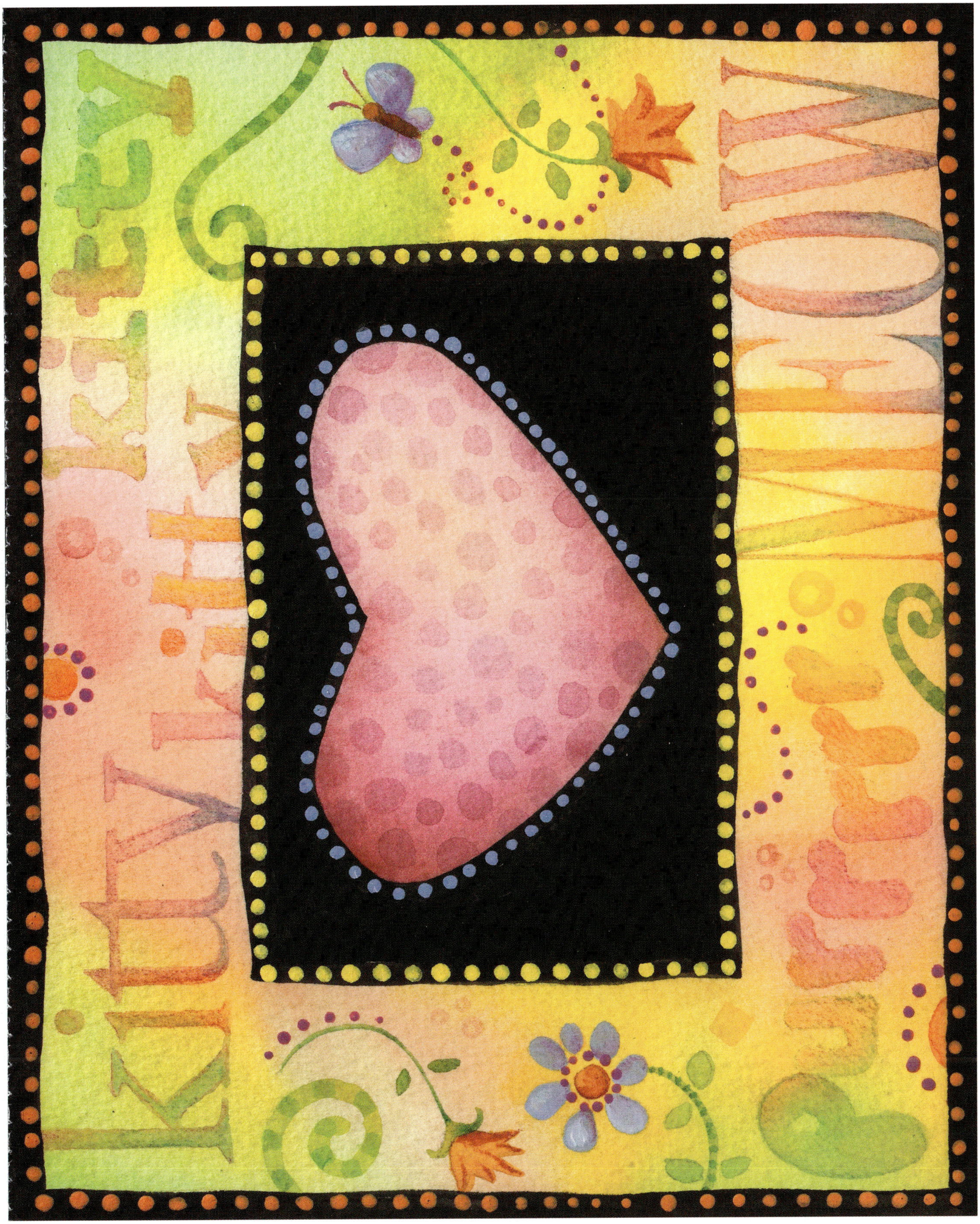
kitty kitty kitty
MEOW

My Cat

used on page 120

puppy
LOVE
best friend
BELOVED
faithful
Loyal
companion

Emma and Honey

used on page 129

Cat Sitter

used on page 121

Cut out frame in the green border area. Trim border strips the same way.

Day in the Field

used on page 125

PHOTO MAT AND
JOURNAL BOX

HEADLINE *(left)*

PHOTO MATS AND JOURNAL BOX

Best Friend

used on pages 126–127

GRADUATION DAY

PHOTO MAT AND LABEL ELEMENTS

PHOTO MAT

PHOTO MAT AND JOURNAL BOXES

CERTIFICATE FOR PERSONALIZATION

Graduation Day

used on page 146

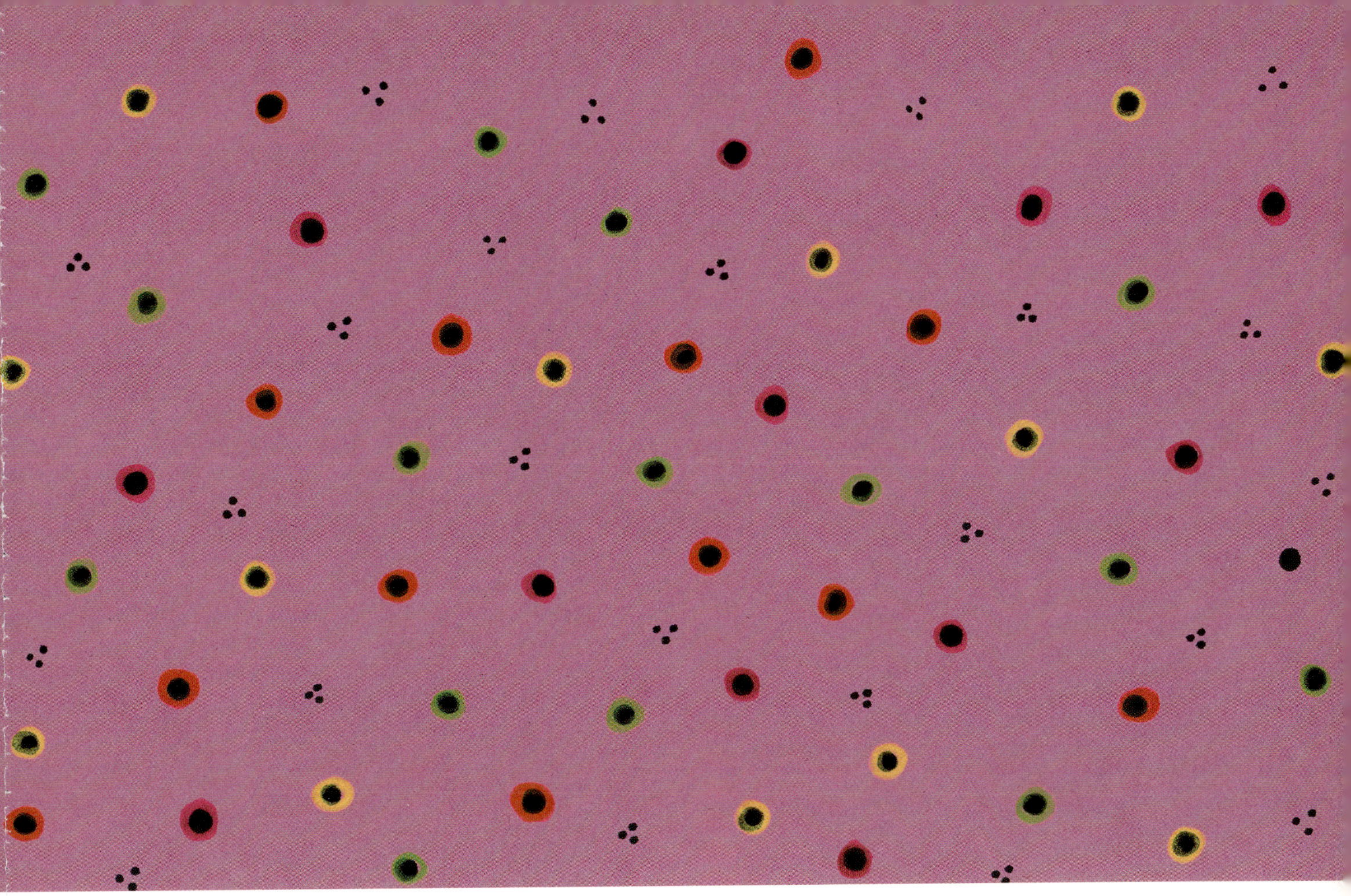

GROUND PAPER

MOON
ART

ALTERNATE
MOONS

Boo

used on page 155

HALLOWEEN ACCENTS OR
PHOTO CORNERS

HAUNTED
HOUSE

Boo

used on page 155

Christmas with Sam

used on pages 162–163

Our Visit with Santa

used on page 171

Idaho Snow

used on pages 176–177

Idaho Snow

used on pages 176–177

To have the wave span 12 inches, photocopy the art at 110 percent. For a facing page photocopy once using a mirror-image setting.

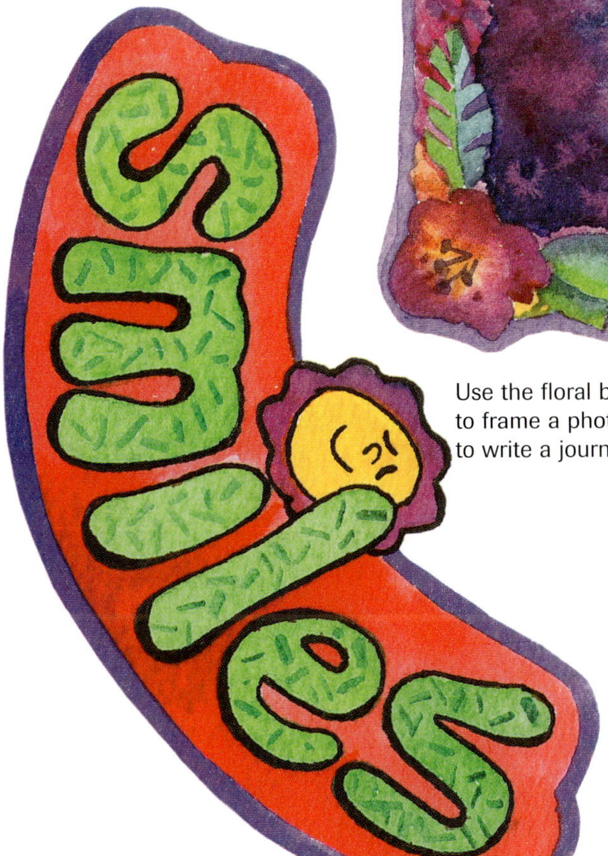

Use the floral border to frame a photo or to write a journal box.

Hawaii Band Trip

used on pages 202–203

Photocopy the tree once on regular setting and once on a mirror-image setting to have two facing palm trees.

Hawaii Band Trip

used on pages 202–203

America the Beautiful

used on pages 222–223

JOURNAL BOX

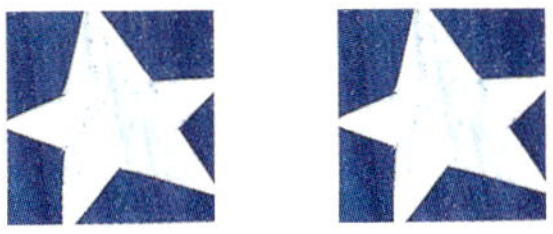

STAR SQUARES

HEADLINE BANNER

HEADLINE BANNER

(right)
PHOTO MAT BAR

(far right)
BORDER STRIP
Enlarge 111 percent for a 12-inch-square page.

America the Beautiful

used on pages 222–223

Marriage Certificate

THIS IS TO CERTIFY

That ______________________________

______________ in the State of ______________

and ______________________ of ______________

in the State of ______________ were by me joined together in

HOLY MATRIMONY

on the ________ day of ______________

in ______________

Witness: ______________ ______________

______________ ______________

MARRIAGE CERTIFICATE — Make three photocopies: For the photo mat on the right-hand page, enlarge to 140 percent; for the vertical floral bands, the headline, and the cutout flowers, enlarge to 220 percent; and for the certificate to personalize on the left-hand page, reduce to 67 percent.

Holy Matrimony

used on pages 240–241

PHOTO MAT

POLKA-DOT TRIANGLES

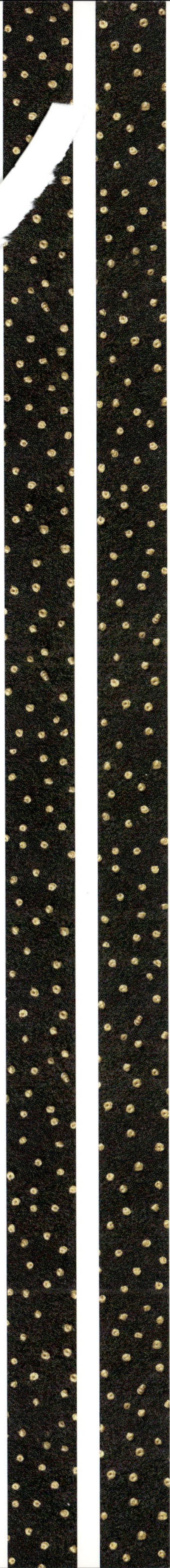

POLKA-DOT BANDS

Holy Matrimony

used on pages 240–241

PHOTO MAT

PHOTO CORNERS

ALTERNATE PHOTO CORNERS

ALTERNATE PHOTO CORNERS

MAT FINIAL

John and Dorothy

used on page 253